PRAISE FOR
HOW TO CREATE YOUR OWN LUCK

"Some people wait and wait for luck to come their way. Others have a knack for creating their own luck. In this inspiring and entertaining book, Susan RoAne reveals the secrets of success- ful people who embrace the You Never Know! philosophy. Since this book has found its way to you, you can let it open your imagination to new life possibilities. Will it change your life? You Never Know!"

Father Paul Keenan
Author, *Good News for Bad Days, Stages of the Soul,* and *Heartstorming*

"The first step in creating your own good luck is to read and practice Susan's sage advice to open yourself to opportunity, expand your network, and take chances. Soon, your life will overflow with abundance and joy."

Michael J. Gelb
Author, *DaVinci Decoded: Discovering the Spiritual Secrets of Leonardo's Seven Principles*

"If you have ever wondered how you could bring more luck into your life, Susan RoAne has the perfect answer. With her trade- mark sense of humor, she distills the stories of real people who turned serendipity and You Never Know! opportunities into suc- cess. She provides insights and a game plan so we can do the same."

Connie Glaser
Best-selling author, *What Queen Esther Knew* and *Swim with the Dolphins*

"The best advice I ever got from my mother was: 'Don't be afraid to ask. The worst they could say is no.' Susan RoAne offers that same kind of straightforward, commonsense approach to creating a life of personal, professional, and spiritual fulfillment. And she does it with love, insight, and humor."

Robert Spector
Author, *The Nordstrom Way*

"There are those people who say 'if only,' and then there are those who ask "what if?' In *How To Create Your Own Luck*, author Susan RoAne gives us the keys to *making* good things happen in life rather than *wishing* they would. The inspiring and practical stories show that if it's "luck," then it's luck of our own making and how we can make the choices that make our dreams come true."

Joe Calloway
Author, *Becoming A
Category Of One*

HOW TO
CREATE
YOUR OWN
LUCK

The "You Never Know" Approach to
Networking, Taking Chances, and
Opening Yourself to Opportunity

SUSAN ROANE

WILEY

John Wiley & Sons, Inc.

Published by John Wiley & Sons, Inc., Hoboken, New Jersey.
Published simultaneously in Canada.

For general information on our other products and services please contact our Customer Care Department within the United States at (800) 762-2974, outside the United States at (317) 572-3993 or fax (317) 572-4002.

Wiley also publishes its books in a variety of electronic formats. Some content that appears in print may not be available in electronic books. For more information about Wiley products, visit our web site at www.Wiley.com.

Library of Congress Cataloging-in-Publication Data:
RoAne, Susan, 1948–
    How to create your own luck : the "you never know" approach to networking, taking chances, and opening yourself to opportunity / Susan RoAne.
        p. cm.
    Includes bibliographical references and index.
    ISBN 0-471-61280-4 (cloth)
  1. Success in business. 2. Social networks. 3. Serendipity. I. Title.
    HF5386.R523 2004
    650.1'3--dc22
2004008611
Printed in the United States of America
10 9 8 7 6 5 4 3 2 1

To my grandmothers, to those who came before us, and to the legions of wise people who are now with us who always answered, "You never know!" when we asked, "Why?" Well, now we know.

CONTENTS

ACKNOWLEDGMENTS

There is no way this book would have been written without the information, assistance, and stories of a lot of amazing people. Writing, in and of itself, is a solitary endeavor, but I was never really alone. Besides the companionship of far too many of Bryan's chocolate chip cookies, my support team was "there" for me. They gave me the room to withdraw and become my author alter ego, "Esther Sequester." And they allowed me to "drop in" as chapters were done and I felt there was a natural break in my work. Writing the acknowledgments is really the best part because it allows me to honor some special folks.

First of all, an incredible thank you to each and every one of my You Never Know It Alls, who shared their stories, their time, and their truths. To David Glickman, who heard me quote my grandmother's saying in my keynote speech in Chicago and came up to me and said, "Susan, You Never Know! is the theme of your next book." I never knew it until he told me. To Michael Gelb who confirmed it. And to Mark Chimsky, who gave me the phrase "expand my brand," the opportunity to teach at New York University's famed Summer Publishing Institute, and the chance to be part of the extended family.

To Mary Haring who had to decipher the scribbling (yes, I still write with No. 2 pencils with good erasers) as well as edit. Thank you for reviewing the book, for brainstorming, and for insightful feedback. To Leigh Bohmfalk, who also helped me enter my tome into the computer. You are troupers.

To Lana Teplick, best friend and "Chief of Staff"—for your decades of "Oh, wows!," wisdom, and laughter.

Joyce Siegel (Mumsy), my Rock of Gibraltar; Carl LaMell, chairman of the board of The RoAne Group; Lois Keenan, Jean Miller, Becky Gordon, Toni Boyle, Dan Maddux, Patricia Fripp, Diane Parente, Connie Glaser (SS1), Laura Fenamore, Kathleen Korth, Simma Lieberman, Barry and Barbara Wishner, Griggs RoAne, and my Saturday sanity circle: Sandy Hufford, Susan Belling, Donna Schafer. Thanks to the team at Recreate, Sherwood and Jonathan Cummins, for keeping me in shape, talking me through the chapters while I pumped iron. To the gang at Bay Club Marin who helped me aerobically dance off those chocolate chip cookies—and lots of steam.

To my clients who have been supportive of my writing and shared their You Never Know! stories along the way.

To my "families": the Skovs, the Berringers, and the Walkers, for including "Grandma Susan" in their lives.

To the Gang at Tully's in Towne Center for lotsa lattes, my "reserved" table, and allowing me to camp out for hours.

To my Mother, Lil, for remembering the details of some wonderful stories, and to my brother, Ira, for a perspective on life that always makes me laugh. And to my dear late grandmothers, who knew that events were *beshert*—meant to be or not meant to be.

To Jon Tandler, publishing attorney and friend—thank you for protection and support. And to Pat Teal, whose advice, support, and friendship have helped me stay the course.

A huge thank you to Airié Stuart, Richard Narramore, Emily Conway, Larry Alexander, and the gang at Wiley, who believe in this book and the value it offers readers. What more could an author want? And to Linda Witzling, my production editor, for her wit, her laughter and warmth, and her skills and insights.

To Michelle Patterson, Lissa Brown, and sales reps for Wiley who work so hard to be sure books are in stores. To the bookstore staffs, the buyers, and hand sellers, thank you, *merci beaucoup, muchas gracias* for over 15 years of your support, efforts, and energy and for always being so nice to me when I popped in during my walks around your cities.

Most of all, my heartfelt thanks to Jessica Papin, who changed my life the day she became my agent. Her wisdom, vision, demeanor, and genuine sweetness, coupled with a terrific sense of humor, have made the journey of this book a pleasure to shop, sell, and write. For the first time in 16 years, I have a partner in the publishing world, and it is joyful. She is an angel.

And to you . . . the book buyers who spread the word— a special *thank-you.* Without you, I wouldn't be an author.

INTRODUCTION

Do you know people who are magnets for new and exciting opportunities? Have you ever wondered how you could catch some of the same lucky breaks? The premise of this book is that most lucky people aren't lucky at all—they simply create their own luck. People who appear to be "in the right place at the right time" are those who have learned to open themselves to opportunity—by keeping open minds, talking to strangers, taking chances, and other key practices I describe in this book. People who create their own luck believe in the "you never know" principle. They scatter the seeds of opportunity everywhere they go and have mastered a set of eight traits that enrich their professional and personal lives.

I've always believed in using the "You Never Know" principle to create my own luck. Here's how I used it to change my career. When the San Francisco school board laid off 1200 teachers, I was one of them. But I was the one who didn't believe George Bernard Shaw's damaging quote about teachers: "Those who can, do; those who can't, teach." I knew that not only could we "do," but that we could "do" better than most. Designing a career change workshop for teachers was my way of helping my colleagues and myself deal with the forced separation from our profession. Could I have planned that the business editor of the *San Francisco Examiner* would catch the last 15 minutes of my radio interview about career change issues and call to ask me if we could do a local weekly career column? I had no way of knowing that saying yes to him, when I had never written a published article and barely had a network of business sources, would result in a weekly column for over three years that would alter my career plans and move me onto my current path as a speaker and author. You never know! I created my own luck by helping my fellow teachers, and by being open to a new opportunity even though I felt unqualified.

A few years later, I wrote a book, *How to Work a Room*®, which was rejected by over 20 publishing houses. My dear friend insisted that I attend the American Library Association's convention to meet potential publishers. I had the flu, felt awful, and said no. But Jean Miller insisted, and then reminded me of the "great opportunity to meet people and make contacts in publishing." I hate hearing my own words repeated back to me, so I reluctantly agreed. She was right. I did meet a publisher who said "yes" to my book, and it went on to sell a million copies. I created my own luck that day by saying "yes" to a networking opportunity when I wanted to say "no."

Many of the people in this book have also experienced situations that were unexpected and evolved from moments of serendipity that they saw as opportunities. Sometimes they embraced positive feedback or good advice or just struck up a conversation with a stranger at a fund-raiser or on a plane. Rather than being immobilized by the rhetorical question "Why?," they are the people who shrug, say "Why not?," and forge ahead. They are everywhere.

Have you ever walked past a parent running with an infant in a jog stroller and thought the stroller was a good idea?

Or heard that an acquaintance was hired for a dream job that you never knew existed?

Or been introduced to a pastry chef making tarts who used to be an attorney filing torts?

Or learned of someone who had been a temporary employee working in the typing pool—and became a vice president in the company?

Or met someone who had to make their own salad dressings because of allergies, then bottled and wrapped them as holiday gifts, found people would pay real money to buy them, and now has a successful business?

You may have thought these people were just lucky and had all the breaks—and they may say the same. "Gosh, I was just lucky" is an easy explanation for what appears to be good fortune. But on closer examination, which I offer in this book, you'll find that luck had very little to do with the success of these people. Those who had "lucky" experiences involving coincidence, happenstance, and timing were, to a one, **open.** In fact, those who are open seem to have many experiences. With great respect and affection, I combined two phrases and call them the You Never Know It Alls. The people you will meet in this book are the role models.

The actions and behaviors of people who create their own luck must not be underestimated—ever. There is much value in our commitment to do hard, smart work, perform the daily tasks, and maintain the "magic of the can-do" positive outlook. There is equal value in the will-ingness to be open—to talk to strangers, make small talk, listen and eavesdrop, give information so that others share information with us, and connect with people in a variety of situations so that we are in the path of unplanned opportunities.

The heroes of this book are people who saw their situations of serendipity and transformed them into something that they believe is success. The corollary is that the rest of us can do the same. But *success* is an all-encompassing word because it means different things to different people. For some, it's all about money. For others, it's the freedom to determine the wheres and whens of working life. And for still others, it's something that contributes to the overall quality of their life.

Although each person exhibited many of the Usual Suspect traits (hard work, persistence, positive attitude, a circle of smart advisors), it is the *Unusual* Suspect traits that provide the extra something that sets the You Never Know It Alls apart. These are the eight (counterintuitive) traits that I share in Chapter 1.

This book contains stories of people like you and I. Some will show how businesses began as a result of a coincidence (kismet, destiny, fate); other stories will highlight how careers evolved or jobs were uncovered. And there are stories of discoveries, inventions, and happy accidents that have met a measure of success. All of the stories incorporate the Create Your Own Luck theme, the perfect explanation for what seems to be the inexplicable: the "meant to be" or "not meant to be" events of life. These true stories vary in length and overlap in the possible category of experience that they represent, although I picked the category most suited to each story.

Each anecdote reflects not only the results of the serendipitous moments, but also the actions and traits utilized when the opportunity appeared. They offer not only "can-do" but also "we can-do it, too" tips. Most chapters include Points to Ponder following the first anecdote, and many of the stories give a brief summary of action steps taken by these gurus of opportunity. For some anecdotes, I have highlighted which of the eight (counter-intuitive) traits they exhibit that contributed to the successful outcome. Many of the chapters also offer exercises that you can choose to do at your leisure.

And what's luck got to do with it?

According to oft-repeated ancient Chinese philosophy, luck is when preparation meets opportunity. We create our own luck when we are prepared to see the opportunities and willing to take action. Contrary to the old cliché, opportunity does not "knock" at our door, but it surrounds us. We just need to be open—like the You Never Know It Alls—who provide a guideline, a game plan, and great inspiration for the rest of us.

THE EIGHT TRAITS

What is it about some people—the ones who create their own luck—that makes them successful? Are they born under a lucky star? Do they get all the breaks? *No!* To a one, they are people who perceive a possibility, see the opportunity, and parlay it into something positive, which has a measure of success. They don't just **see** opportunity, they **seize** it. They are observers who pay attention—to issues, to problems, to perplexing situations, and to people. Regardless of whether their moment of serendipity turns into a job or business or two tickets to the Olympics or the opera, they are *open* to it!

The stories of these people reveal that they fall into two categories:

- **The Usual Suspects:** When studying the stories that changed people's careers, jobs, or businesses, there is a track of traits I mentioned in the Introduction called the Usual Suspects. Discussed in most business books, these are the qualities and characteristics generally ascribed to those who are successful. These people don't just work smart, they work hard

rather than hardly work! They cultivate a good attitude. Some days their outlook is realistic, other days
it's simply positive, but whichever it is, their attitude
is a healthy one that embraces possibility. In addition, they have a vision that is bolstered by great
follow-through.

- **The *Unusual* Suspects:** What most business books
and courses don't identify are the unique traits
exhibited by people who have seized the serendipity,
co-opted the coincidence, and captured the karma.
These Unusual Suspect traits set such people apart
from the crowd, incorporating **counterintuitive** behaviors, actions, and attitudes that go against the
prescribed norm. Interestingly enough, these traits
are also the outgrowth of solid, savvy networking
skills.

People who successfully create their own luck exhibit
different combinations of these eight traits:

Trait One: They talk to strangers.
Trait Two: They make small talk.
Trait Three: They drop names.
Trait Four: They eavesdrop and listen.
Trait Five: They ask for or offer help.
Trait Six: They stray from their chosen paths.
Trait Seven: They exit graciously without burning
   bridges.
Trait Eight: They say yes when they want to say no.

These You Never Know It Alls don't conform to the
"keep it to yourself and play your cards close to your vest"
school of thought. They remain open, and that openness
is the linchpin of their so-called luck.

First and foremost, the people featured in this book talk to people they don't know.

TRAIT ONE: TALK TO STRANGERS

Introduced in my book *How to Work a Room*® (1988) as an antidote to the warning "Don't talk to strangers," this counterintuitive trait opened up a world of possibilities for most of the people in this book. If you take a moment to think about it, you have had an experience that started with talking to someone you didn't know. Such incidental, serendipitous conversations can sometimes score huge successes and make a dramatic impact on the bottom line.

A Royal Crown Room

Although we now complain about the inconveniences of cross-country business travel, the reality is that there have always been travails of travel that try our patience: flight delays, canceled flights, long layovers. Although merely annoying for the pleasure traveler, such unforeseen circumstances can mean a disaster for the businessperson who misses a meeting, presentation, or client conference.

One of those flight delays was aggravating for Mark Mayberry, a professional speaker, consultant, and author. "I had planned my travel perfectly. But sometimes the weather gods don't cooperate, and I was facing a long delay. Fortunately, I am a Delta Crown Club member and just figured I would go to the club, have a beverage, do some work, and read my book. Some other passengers were quite agitated, but I figured there was nothing I could do . . . might as well relax.

"As I sat down, I struck up a conversation with another

fellow, who was also delayed. We had a few things in common: We were on our way somewhere, members of the Crown Club, and very frequent fliers. We were both agitated because a golf tournament that was on TV was not on a channel available in the Crown Club. That's what started our conversation. We shared a few golf stories and had a few laughs. It was very casual and a pleasant way to pass the time. When our flight was called we said goodbye and wished each other well. No big deal. Was I ever wrong!

"I got on the plane and knew I was wasting a good opportunity and decided that was not an option. In the course of our conversation I had learned he was just named president of Atlantic Southeast Airlines. So I walked up to him and made sure I had his contact information and sent him my book. Then I followed up a little later. The result of this coincidental meeting and incidental conversation was two contracts totaling more than a half million dollars to consult with his company. It was the most lucrative weather delay of my career."

Striking up a conversation with a stranger isn't always easy. Shared circumstances can make it easier for us to do that. Mark could have behaved in an irritated and unpleasant manner. He could have become so irate that he kept to himself. Or he could have made bitter, whining remarks to that stranger in the airport club, stopping the conversation cold. There was nothing at stake, so it was just a pleasant interchange between two strangers in the same place at the same time, who wished they could watch a golf tournament. It was serendipitous that they were seated close enough to chat. However, Mark's willingness to see and seize the opportunity to chat with someone who turned out to be the *perfect* stranger (as in a six-figure client) made all the difference. What's most important is that he made sure he could make contact again, send his book, and follow up with a phone call.

Mark scored a huge business success, but sometimes "lucky" breaks successfully score things of a different nature—such as tickets to opening night at the opera.

TRAIT TWO: MAKE SMALL TALK

In my travels across the country giving presentations, I have learned that many people hold small talk in low regard. While researching *What Do I Say Next?* (Warner Books, 1999), I discovered that the people who put down small talk are generally those who are bad at it. Those who are adept, **the ConverSENsations**® described in that book, see small talk as a way to get to know people, and thus they never denigrate it.

People who create their own luck don't wait for a great opening line, nor do they initiate conversation with big talk—about such daunting topics as famine in underdeveloped countries, quantum theory in physics, or the social cost of incarcerating first-time offenders. Although these are terrific big talk topics, the people who attract coincidental opportunities tend to talk about little things: weather, traffic, movies, and the like. They might start by saying, "Hello, how are you?" And then they **listen** to the answer.

Diane Parente, an in-demand image and wardrobe specialist and founder of the Association of Image Consultants International, was taking her morning swim before work at a club in San Francisco. She was running a little late when she spotted one of her clients getting into the pool.

"I was in a hurry, but I felt it would be rude to just say hello and turn around and walk away." Diane, a genuinely open person and a great conversationalist, chatted at length with Jill, her client.

"As I was about to leave, Jill said she had to go out of town that weekend and asked me if we could use her two tickets to opening night at the San Francisco Opera. I was ecstatic. My husband, Lou, and I are great fans of the opera, but opening night tickets are almost as hard to get as tickets for the Super Bowl."

Small talk yielded a big payoff for the Parentes because *La Traviata* is one of their favorites. But people who create their own luck are not one-trick ponies.

"When we arrived at the opera, we were in orchestra seats next to a couple who were women's clothing designers in New York, and I was familiar with their work. We just started to chat with them. During intermission, the wife indicated she wasn't feeling well. Her husband turned to us and asked if we could use their tickets to the Gala Ball following the opera. We were speechless. Fortunately, we were able to say yes, and thank you."

If Diane and Lou Parente had not exchanged light-hearted conversation with these people, they never would have attended opening night at the San Francisco Opera and the Gala Ball. Some of Diane's clients were season opera subscribers, and she was able to connect with them on another level, apart from their business relationship.

A Plane Lesson on Snobbery

The importance of being open, talking to strangers, and making small talk hit home like a sledgehammer for Ed Peters, a sales trainer, who logs many frequent-flier miles. One doesn't have to be a baseball fan to share in the lesson Ed learned the hard way.

"Little did I know that the flight from San Francisco to Chicago in October of 1984 would change my life forever. It was a Friday, the end of a long, exhausting work week in San Francisco. I wasn't exactly excited about a four-hour flight home to Chicago, but at least I had been upgraded to a first-class seat . . . in which I planned to sleep all the way back home. Making small talk was not part of my plane plan.

"No sooner am I sitting down than I hear a booming voice, 'How you doing?' My thought was, 'With my luck, that guy will have the seat next to me.'

" 'I asked, how you doing?' he yelled one more time as he crawled across me and landed in the seat right next to me. In between my thinking that I wasn't going to get any sleep and that this guy would want to talk all the way to Chicago, he shouted out, "Hi, I'm Ernie." I didn't even look at him.

"There is one other empty seat in first class and it's next to the guy across the aisle from me. I'm thinking how lucky he is to get an empty seat next to him when up walks a beautiful woman who sits in that empty seat. I was tired, exasperated, and a bit jealous.

"So this guy gets this beautiful woman, and I've got . . . Ernie. Meanwhile I hear the woman across the aisle tell her seatmate she was a *Playboy* Playmate of the Month and was on her way to Chicago for her centerfold photo shoot. This guy's got a Playboy Playmate, and I've got . . . Ernie. I did my best to ignore Ernie by putting on my headphones, but it didn't deter him.

"When we landed, I got off the plane very quickly, ducked into the nearest restroom, and bumped into the guy who sat across the aisle. He asked me, 'So, are you and Ernie good friends?' 'Yeah right,' I said sarcastically. Then he said, 'Man, I would have given anything to have been able to spend four hours sitting next to *Mr.* Cub, Ernie Banks!'

"My jaw dropped in disbelief, and I slinked out of the restroom thinking, 'I just sat next to Ernie Banks, one of my all-time favorite baseball heroes and I completely blew the best coincidence of a lifetime because I didn't give him the time of day, much less exchange small talk.'

"If I'm such a huge baseball fan, how was it I didn't know I was sitting next to Ernie Banks? I didn't want to make eye contact so I never looked at him."

Ed believes that in 1984 he learned the ultimate lesson in networking. Now he talks to everybody! Ed learned that if you respond to strangers, open up and make small talk with them, and, better yet, *listen* to them, good things happen. This true story changed his outlook, his behavior, and his life—especially his business life.

"I've come to realize that all business starts with a relationship, and that relationships start with communication. Since that fateful plane ride with Ernie Banks, I've never underestimated that business is all around us if we are open to that possibility . . . and embrace the opportunities that present themselves.

"I learned not to let 'prime times' become 'slime times' and that to be open to the world of possibilities that exists can make your business profitable and your life pleasurable beyond your wildest dreams."

For someone who grew up in Chicago like I did, Ernie Banks is a hero: *Mr. Cub.* My brother and several of my friends would trade their first- and second-born children to spend even an hour in the presence of the Great One. Ed Peters will always remember how he blew this serendipitous situation. To his credit, he learned a lesson and was willing to let us learn from his mistake as well.

You can change and control your own luck by making time for the casual conversation we call small talk. Much like the ConverSENsations I observed in *What Do I Say Next?*, open people are not dismissive of small talk. As Michael Korda writes in *Power* (Random House, 1975), they see small talk as a way to get to know people—and that often leads to Big Talk.

Small talk might start with an exchange of information about kids, pets, food, parents, sports, books, or yes, even the weather (it happens to all of us). Small talk can take place at a party, at the opera, at the watercooler, at a fund-raiser, at a bookstore, on the golf course, or in line at the supermarket. The best listeners and eavesdroppers are empathic, a quality that allows them to form deeper connections.

TRAIT THREE: DROP NAMES

As I sat at the table at the historic Old Ebbett Grill on a very hot and humid summer day in D.C., I looked across at my young companion and thought how unlikely it was that we would have spent a day together at the Corcoran Gallery and having lunch. That this lovely 20-year-old college coed would even want to hang with me was amazing, as she had met me only once and I was older than her parents. But when her mother, Jody Pilka, received my e-mail about my pending visit, she realized that she would be on a business trip and that her husband had a meeting. She mentioned my invite for lunch and a museum tour, and daughter Courtney volunteered. How this came about is just one of the "small world" stories that have added spice to my life.

It started four years earlier, when I received the web site inquiry from a potential client who wanted to discuss a presentation, based on my books. The inquiry was very businesslike, although I took special notice of her last name. When Jody, a vice president of Ryan Homes, and I finally spoke, she mentioned that her office was in Gaithersburg, Maryland. "Oh, I have a sister-in-law there," I commented, connecting with Jody on a more personal level.

We discussed the usual: how she found me and read my books, the agenda and objectives for the two-day meeting for sales staff, when and where it would take place. The exchange was pleasant, and our conversational energies matched, but I knew she was interviewing other speakers as well.

At the end of the conversation, I decided to take a risk and ask a personal question. "Jody, are you from Chicago?"

"No, but my husband's family is."

"Really? Were they in the paper business?"

"I think his grandfather was."

It was time to drop the big name. There is a school of thought that says dropping names is a way of showing off. If I were to mention that I had just been at a party with some big muckety-muck, it would be offensive. But this was different. There was a connection between us, and I had to let her know.

"Please sit down," I warned Jody. "Is your husband's grandfather Ike?"

Her surprise was apparent in her voice. "How did you know?"

"Jody, my dad worked for your husband's grandfather for 26 years . . . then bought the company."

Jody responded with surprise, excitement, and disbelief. Out of nowhere, she has contacted an author to speak to her company and discovers a connection to the Pilka family. I was a link to their past, and she was a link to mine.

E-mails and phone calls followed, establishing the reconnection. My parents had been guests at her husband's parents' wedding, and his grandparents were at my parents' wedding. My mother even remembered the gift they gave to her and my dad.

Yes, I was chosen to speak at the programs for Jody's company. But there was an extra bonus. I spent the weekend in Baltimore and from there drove out to Virginia to visit with Jody, her husband, Eric, and their daughters in order to meet the family of the man I grew up hearing so much about. Eric's grandfather was part of the lore of the Randolph Paper Company.

Jody and I stay in touch and have seen each other on subsequent occasions. None of that would have happened had I not risked sounding foolish with a potential client by dropping the name we had in common. Jody's openness to my questions is what enabled us to connect. At any point in our conversation she could have shut things down by saying "No, I am not from Chicago" or "No, my husband's family is not in the paper business." She could have done a Dragnet—"Just the facts, ma'am"—and then hastily ended the conversation. But she didn't.

Jody's response was not monosyllabic or terse; she took the time to elaborate, which established what we had in common. This certainly impacted my business in a positive way, but it also brought a lot of joy and fond memories to Eric's stepmom, who knew my parents, and to my mother, who adored Ike Pilka.

Dropping the names of people, places, and events that you might have in common with a stranger creates connections that open the door to opportunity.

Life is like that.

TRAIT FOUR: EAVESDROP AND LISTEN

People who benefit from coincidence and serendipity not only listen and observe, but also have highly refined *overhearing* skills. An episode of the television show *Frasier* reinforces the traditional lesson that it is not nice to eavesdrop. Dr. Crane overhears a bit of news and is told by his very sensible father, a former policeman, that "overhearing is like wiretaps, inadmissible in court."

However, for the savvy communicator, keeping one's ears open is a way to court information, to learn, assess, and get a feel for the market. Listening and overhearing are ways to do very low cost "market research," although you may end up getting more direction than you bargained for. There are benefits to being the eavesdropper, but also to being the one who is eavesdropped on.

Tapped Out: A Success for Body and Soul

Sharon, a small business owner, had started her aerobics studio more than two decades earlier, and had been one of the first in the area. However, now her business was in trouble. The rent at the shopping center in which it was located had skyrocketed, and Sharon now faced competition from major health clubs and studios that had not existed when she was the "first on her block"—and for miles around. Body and Soul began losing clients to full-service health clubs.

As her clients aged and their needs changed, Sharon focused her efforts on senior prime-time classes. Although getting new clients was hard, she had a loyal base of customers who had been with her for many of her twenty years in business.

Sharon did have a subrenter, a dance company, that made it possible to keep the doors of her studio open. When this longtime subrenter moved to a new location, things began to look bleak. She was on the verge of having to close her studio after twenty years.

Bonnie Alexander had been teaching tap at the local recreation and park center. "I never thought that the current studio was very amenable. One day, after attending an exercise class, I **overheard** Sharon on the phone saying that she had lost her subtenant. I waited till she was alone so I would not risk embarrassing her or spill the beans in front of other students. I told Sharon what I had heard, and that I thought her studio was in a great location for our tap and ballet classes. It was well lit for night classes, it had unlimited parking, and it had a great sound system and even a piano. Plus, I had always enjoyed the aerobics classes at Body and Soul and wanted to continue having it available. Sharon was very interested.

"I mentioned the studio to my colleague, who taught the ballet and jazz dance classes in the students' program. It just seemed like the perfect option for both of our classes. It would solve Sharon's problem, and we would have a much better facility. Little did I know that a week after I had started the ball rolling, the studio that the Rec and Park Department was using would be condemned and closed! It was amazing serendipity that the solution was in progress before we knew that there was a real problem. The timing was more perfect than I could have planned.

"Because it involved city codes, board votes, and some politicizing, the final decision took longer than we would have preferred. But it did happen. Our ballet, tap, and hula dance classes now take place in a lovely studio. Our students have made the transition of location very easily. The parents prefer the location because it is in one of the shopping centers, and that makes it easy for them. They get to do their grocery shopping, errands, or have a cup of Peet's coffee until the class is over."

And Sharon's business is no longer in danger of losing its lease.

Getting a new market for a stand-alone aerobics studio is difficult when it is surrounded by newer full-service clubs. Without investors, it's almost impossible. But you never know when a customer, familiar with the situation the business is facing, might be able to step in and save the day. There are many stories in which a community saves a local small business when the big guys move into town. The business might be a bookstore, a coffeehouse, the local shoe repair shop, or the ice cream parlor—but a little nostalgia, some shared information, and loyal customers can make a big difference.

As a result of Bonnie Alexander's overhearing Sharon's phone call approaching her with a proposed solution, Sharon was able to face her problem and overcome it. Bonnie's actions helped save a longtime small business from closing its doors. In this case, a bit of eavesdropping, some matchmaking, the superb timing of serendipity, and, as Bonnie says, "my big mouth" were the tools that turned a potential disaster into a "small business saved" success story.

TRAIT FIVE: ASK FOR OR OFFER HELP

So many of us were raised with the old adage about making it on our own—not asking for help but instead "pulling ourselves up by our bootstraps." That may work for some, but people who create their own luck are willing to do what novelist E. Lynn Harris did.

Harris spent 13 years selling computers for a major blue-chip company. But his heart was set on writing a novel. In a *San Francisco Chronicle* article, by Adair Lara, Harris said, "I always knew words could change people's lives. I'd go to the library when I was younger. I knew there was a big world waiting for me."[1]

He quit his job and moved to Atlanta to write his novel. Because he could not sell it to any publisher, he self-published it. But bookstores weren't willing to take on his book.

"I knew from selling computers, it takes sales to get people's attention," Harris said. So he **asked** friends to throw book parties featuring his novel, and he asked owners of small businesses with predominantly African-American clienteles whether he could leave copies of his books in their shops.

"I'd leave a copy in beauty salons with a note reading 'Please don't remove.' " People who had begun reading his book while waiting their turn in the chair started to call him with orders.

"One day a woman called me from Doubleday publishing who happened to read one of these self-published copies. She said it was 'one of the most enjoyable reading experiences' and asked if I had an agent."

When Harris went to see literary agent John Hawkins, he took a copy of his book and also mentioned the woman from Doubleday. Although Harris had thought she might be a secretary, he learned from Hawkins that she was actually a powerful person in the publishing world named Martha Levin. Hawkins then asked Harris whether he could represent him.

E. Lynn Harris is now a *New York Times* best-selling author who has sold over 3 million books. He had a passion and a plan and was willing to ask for help. The combination of his knowledge of his community and the sales process yielded a series of coincidences and sweet serendipity that catapulted him to the pinnacle at which he finds himself today.

TRAIT SIX: STRAY FROM THE PATH

Some very successful individuals follow paths they chose deliberately and for which they trained or attended school, or in which they had experience. But others exemplify a counterintuitive trait, and these people did not stay on the expected course. When the "Aha" light-bulb lit up, they allowed themselves to detour from their paths in order to pursue the new ones that had been illuminated for them. Such a fork in the road beckons these people down a new path in life.

We all make choices based on a variety of factors:

research and advice, family and peer pressure, and sheer gut reactions. The unpredictable result can fall into the "You Never Know!" category. We travel roads that have led us, albeit circuitously, to the place where we are. What if we had (or had not) taken that proverbial fork in the road that, as Robert Frost famously said, "has made all the difference"?

When Jansen Chan was a little boy, his father taught him to bake. When he was in primary school, Jansen and his dad would bake cakes for birthdays, parties, anniversaries, and traditional Chinese celebrations. They considered the foundation, design, structure, and, of course, the ingredients and taste of their cakes. The presentation was part of the planning process. Jansen was ten years old when his father succumbed to cancer after a seven-year battle, but Jansen's memories of baking with his dad remained strong as he grew older.

Jansen had a general interest in design, structure, and form as well as visual presentation, so after his high school graduation, he planned to explore those interests at the University of California, Berkeley, in the school of architecture. He was an excellent student, who completed the five-year course and found a job as an architect with a local firm.

As Jansen tells it, "For two years, I worked on design projects and structures and discovered that I didn't like working as an architect." The path Jansen had not chosen called to him from a place deep within his most cherished memories. He broke the news to his employers and to his mother and left the firm. "I had to see if the path I didn't originally pursue was the one I wanted," he said.

Jansen arranged to apprentice to the pastry chef at a downtown restaurant rather than attend culinary school. His love of art—designing, paying attention to detail, and creating eye-pleasing edible structures (desserts)—prevailed. He worked at a four-star restaurant as the assistant pastry chef and was part of the team that created the Pecan Marjolaine with Julia's Chocolate Mousse for Julia Child's ninetieth birthday celebration. He followed his dream by returning to his preferred path—and found it to be the right one.

What did his mother, a chief development officer in the public school system, say about his career change? "At first I was surprised and a little disappointed. Now I see how happy he is, how good he is at what he does, and that makes me happy."

Jansen is currently in training with Alain Ducasse to work at Mix in Las Vegas. "I now love what I do, although it requires a lot of hard work and standing on your feet for ten hours a day. It's not lucrative, but it's my passion."

Jansen set out to follow the prescribed path, studying architecture in a traditional academic setting. He gave it a fair chance and worked in the field while he learned the machinations of the market, the business, and the politics. But he also learned that he did *not* like it.

Jansen took a risk by leaving an established and well-respected profession. He also risked disappointing his mother. However, he had the courage to pay attention to the "voice inside." To make this career switch, he had to network in a brand-new arena in search of a pastry chef willing to mentor him. He also had to learn a whole new set of aesthetic details, work procedures, business policies, and office politics in his new profession. But it made him happy, and continues to do so.

TRAIT SEVEN: TIMELY, GRACIOUS EXITS WITHOUT BURNING BRIDGES

Newspapers and magazines often carry stories about sports figures, entertainers, and executives who leave their careers at their peak. They know "when to hold 'em, and when to fold 'em." Perhaps Shakespeare said it best: "All's well that ends well."

Jerry Seinfeld wanted to leave at the top of his game because he felt that too many television series stay too long at the fair. In a recent interview, Ray Romano, of the sitcom *Everybody Loves Raymond,* echoed this desire to exit his series before it becomes stale. He wants to avoid the fate of "the Fonz" from the sitcom *Happy Days*, who was forced to "jump the shark"—a reference to the extreme plot gimmicks TV writers resort to in order to maintain ratings once a show is past its prime.

Tennis star Pete Sampras, winner of five U.S. Opens and seven Wimbledon championships, was honored at the U.S. Open in 2003. He was officially retiring at the age of 36 from the game he loved. Sampras was one of the greats both on the court and off the court—a gentleman who is admired by his fans, the press, and his colleagues. The tribute to him at the U.S. Open reflected his most gracious and timely exit.

After her Farewell Tour, Cher explained, "You have to stop when you're really good at it." It's the preconcert hustle and staging that wear her down, according to a *USA Today* article by Edna Gunderson. "Performing is the easy part. The hard part is going from hotel to hotel, venue to venue. It's strenuous and backbreaking." At 56, Cher wants to "exit gracefully before rust sets in."[2]

A gracious and timely exit can prevent you from burning your bridges. And why is this important? Because you just never know!

On Her Toes: Salvaging a Burnt Bridge

Marika Sakellariou's careers have combined her passion for ballet with her commitment to fitness and excellence in sports. But it was her gracious, carefully considered, and well-choreographed conversation with Maestro Kurt

Herbert Adler—after he fired her—that was Marika's turning point.

"I was a little girl living in my native Greece when my best school friend invited me to come to a class with her," Marika says. "I was excited, as I thought I was going to her gymnastics class and would get to do cartwheels. My best friend was Finnish and she spoke no Greek; I spoke no Finnish. When I walked into the 'gymnastics class,' I found a very different class: ballet. But the minute I heard the music, I fell in love with the dance.

"I worked very hard in ballet. One day my ballet teacher, Miss Laine Metz, said she was getting too old to demonstrate the steps. She said I could earn my classes by learning all of the ballet terminology and ballet exercises and teaching them to the students. She ended up closing her studio and becoming my mentor and advocate in the ballet world."

Marika and her family moved to Canada, where she became involved in sports and was an Olympic gymnastics competitor. She attended Connecticut College for Women and Juilliard, and started her own ballet company in Marin County, California—the Marin Repertory Dance Theater.

Marika continues, "One day, Mr. Kurt Herbert Adler of the San Francisco Opera, known as a demanding and formidable maestro, saw a performance of my company. We later learned that the Opera Ballet was having an audition, and my partner thought that I should go with him to try out. Although I knew it would interfere with my dance company and wanted to refuse, I agreed and was hired as a soloist.

"On a day my dance company had a scheduled performance, I was supposed to dance a solo and, luckily, the choreographer of SFOB [San Francisco Opera Ballet] agreed that I would not appear and could be with my dance company. But when Mr. Adler noticed I wasn't on stage, he fired me! I was very upset because I had permission to be absent, which he did not know. I felt I had to speak to him and requested a meeting. I was quite nervous, but I calmly told him that my absence was authorized—and added that if he didn't know that, then there was no administrative leadership.

"I was twenty-three at the time and to say what I did to Maestro Adler could have been career suicide. It took more guts than I thought I had. He paused, and asked me who he should hire to provide that leadership. I thought about it, looked him in the eye, and said, 'Me.' He asked me to write a proposal describing the position I would fill. He accepted it. I stayed for 10 years, choreographed over 40 ballets, and designed a fitness regime for the dancers in the off-season.

"After a ballet injury, I became more involved in sports fitness and became a licensed fitness instructor. I designed Enduradance™ as a training [method] for Olympic athletes."

Under the umbrella of her company, Marikasport, she also invented the Ski-slide to prepare U.S. gold medalist Jonny Mosley for the 1998 Winter Olympics. The Ski-slide exercise method won a Nike Innovation Award and was licensed to Reebok. "I continue to teach ballet, combining my first love with my passion for fitness," Marika comments.

Avoiding the burning of bridges is not about being meek or allowing yourself to become a victim. It's about being professional and reasonable. Marika was unfairly fired and had every right to be furious and resentful; instead, she chose to handle the situation with a combination of tact, grace, and chutzpah. Because she had the courage to speak to Maestro Adler with respect and graciousness, Marika salvaged a bridge that was almost burnt for her, and the rest is ballet history.

Not burning bridges is a common trait of people who

create their own luck, but being able to reconstruct one that has been burnt for you is an act of grace.

An untimely exit as the result of a layoff, a merger, or cost-cutting measures can be a disruptive and unexpected experience. While we can't control company decisions, we can control our response to them. A gracious exit can ensure that you will get a good letter of recommendation or some work as an independent contractor— or even that you will be rehired in the future. But a bitter end guarantees that none of these are possibilities.

People whose opportunities have been transformed into successes have often benefited from their own good behavior. When the CEO of Clearbrook, Carl LaMell, interviewed two final candidates for a senior executive position, he asked both when they could start. One fellow said he could start the following Monday. The other said it would take a month, because he had projects to finish and couldn't leave his present employer in the lurch. The staff assumed Carl would choose the first candidate. "Not at all," Carl explained. "Why would I want someone who would leave a position with four days' notice? If he would do that to his current boss, he'd do that to us. I didn't want to hire someone who could leave a position so lightly and not care about burning bridges."

TRAIT EIGHT: SAY YES WHEN YOU WANT TO SAY NO

A current trend, recommended as a time management technique, is to just say *no* to anything that might be an imposition on our time. However, the corollary is that we are also saying no to any opportunities that might result if we had said yes.

Some people's lives constitute a series of serendipitous events. These people live large and embrace life. Today

Anna Maria Bertacchi is executive administration manager of United Nations Federal Credit Union because many years earlier she said yes when she really had wanted to say no.

Anna Maria has an infectious smile that lights up a room. It caught the eye of an older woman in her church who seemed to be alone most of the time. When she began to smile back, Anna Maria would say hello and ask her how she was.

"After a few months of our growing conversations," says Anna Maria, "she asked me if I would drive her to Wednesday night Bible study. I was a bit surprised and speechless because I didn't often go to that class.

"But I felt honored that she would ask me out of everyone at the church. And I thought Elizabeth was alone. Even though it was not something I planned to attend regularly, instead of doing the sensible thing and saying no, I heard myself say, 'Sure, I'll take you.'

"Over the course of time, we became close. She knew I lived near my family home and helped to care for my dad, who had been an invalid since I was 10 years old. The year following my dad's death was a time of great change for me. I began to work at a struggling community hospital in the public relations and development office. I also wanted to go to school and get a bachelor's degree. During that year, Elizabeth decided to sell her home and move to Phoenix to be near her son. As I helped her pack, she made me promise two things: to visit her and to get my degree. I was determined to keep both those promises. I just couldn't figure out how to work and go to school.

"Then I remembered that years earlier, when I was working as a secretary at IBM in New York, I had won an award that was presented at a conference in the Los Angeles area. As I was sitting on the beach, staring at the

Pacific Ocean, I knew that it was my destiny to move there. I went home, told my supervisor, and asked for a transfer to the California office."

After two years, Anna Maria sensed that her family needed her back in New York. She spent her last few months in California working as a temporary secretary for a supervisor who was pursuing a weekend college degree program at Loyola Marymount. She encouraged Anna Maria to do the same and mentioned Marymount College in Tarrytown, New York, which offered the same weekend degree program. Although she had never heard of the program, Anna Maria had grown up in Tarrytown.

"Years later, after I had promised Elizabeth I would go to college, I remembered this conversation and enrolled in the program. I still worked at a local hospital doing PR, volunteered at church, and continued my friendship with Elizabeth.

"Three years into the program, I began to feel so tired and discouraged. One evening, when Elizabeth called, I became very emotional and said that I wanted to give up. A couple of weeks later, Elizabeth's son contacted me and asked me how much it would cost for me to get my degree. He said that his mom had spoken with him and they decided that they wanted to pay my way through college. I was shocked.

"Shortly after that conversation, I received a check for $10,000 to cover the cost of my courses and a new computer. And two years later, at the age of 36, I marched across the stage and received my bachelor's in psychology with honors.

"After I got my degree, I looked for a new job and saw an ad for a company in Manhattan that was looking for a PR specialist. The job involved international relations, and required a college degree, which I now had. I began working for the United Nations Federal Credit Union. I have organized a grand opening of our office in Geneva, Switzerland, and traveled to Germany and Rome, where we made presentations to the U.N. staff. As I stood on the balcony of my hotel overlooking the Coliseum, I thought, Wow! I had come a long way.

"If I had said no to Elizabeth, who wanted to attend Bible study, instead of yes, I would not have had this incredible series of opportunities or met the sweet woman who changed my entire life."

Volunteers in professional associations are frequently asked to donate their time and talents. Sometimes saying yes instead of no to such requests can make an impact on your life in a way you never imagined. Jennifer Klein was involved in her local Sacramento chapter of the Public Relations Society of America when she was asked to do yet another task for their annual holiday event.

"I had so much on my plate, between client work, holiday obligations, and my other responsibilities for the organization that one more thing seemed like the last straw. But I had been a member since I was a student at U.C. Davis, and everyone had been so helpful to me in my career that I just thought it wouldn't kill me to meet with the celebrity emcee. Sander Walker was a D.J. at our local radio station not too far from my office. So I arranged to meet with him to deliver the script.

"As we went over the event's agenda and script, we ended up having a great time, talking and laughing a lot."

And they still are having a great time. Jennifer and Sander turned their serendipitous meeting into a success by my (and every matchmaker's) standards. They married and are now the parents of Jayde Anne.

Consider the possibilities of saying yes to something when you really want to say no. Doing this in your business life can have a major impact on your personal life as well.

RoAne's Reminders

The eight counterintuitive traits that we've discussed are what set apart the "lucky" ones from the rest of us. Their behaviors and actions transformed those experiences we generally refer to as coincidence, kismet, karma, fate, destiny, or luck from serendipity into success. Once again, here are the eight characteristics that made all the difference for the people we met in this chapter:

- Talk to strangers.
- Make small talk.
- Drop names.
- Eavesdrop and listen.
- Ask for or offer help.
- Stray from chosen paths.
- Exit graciously without burning bridges.
- Say yes instead of no.

People who create their own luck live large, remain **open to possibility,** and **expect** that good things will happen—and they *do.* You will be able to identify at least one, and often more, of these eight traits in the "lucky people" whose stories are told in this book.

Think about the events, the opportunities, and the coincidences that are taking place in your life right now. Maybe a door is closing, but there is a window that can be pried open. For example, you might be feeling burned out on the job when a friend suggests that you talk to his former boss, who is starting a company. The first step is to recognize the opportunity, then evaluate it for its potential.

What can you do now to transform these possibilities into opportunities with positive outcomes?

A Closer Look at the Current Opportunities in Your Life

Opportunity

1. You are invited to join the board of a highly regarded not-for-profit organization.

Action Plan

- Interview current board members.
- Assess time commitment and responsibilities.
- Attend a meeting and/or event.

2.

3.

4.

5.

Once you are open, you will hear, see, and simply bump into more opportunities that you can add to the list.

LEMONS TO LEMONADE

'You never know' is an expression I have heard all my life from family, friends, colleagues, classmates, clients, and even out of my own mouth. It covers so much: the coincidence, the serendipity, even caution about what to say in public because "You never know who will hear . . . and who their relatives or friends are." Of course, growing up in Chicago adds an "interesting" layer to that warning. But it still serves me well.

I have a term for people who constantly open themselves to opportunity; I call them "You Never Know It Alls." When we are open, we can see possibilities, seize them and transform them into valuable—and sometimes amusing—experiences.

The title of this chapter, "Lemons to Lemonade" is an expression that is still in the vernacular. We've heard it and, most likely, have used it to describe the bad situation that turned into a positive result. Most You Never Know It Alls have had these sour lemon situations in their lives: a layoff, a life plan gone awry, or a business that folds. By being open and seeing opportunity, and with some persistence and resilience, they turn that lemon into lemonade.

As you read their stories, you will be able to recognize which of the eight counterintuitive traits helped these people become You Never Know It Alls and enabled them to transform serendipity into success.

While getting fired for just cause is troublesome, getting laid off as the result of a company's cost-saving measures is just as unsettling. Some people search for a new job, but others find a new way to work—for themselves.

OOPS! OUR PINK SLIPS ARE SHOWING!

Arlynn Greenbaum worked in the public relations/ publicity department at a publishing house. As she tells it, "I loved being part of the world of publishing and enjoyed creating and implementing publicity campaigns for authors. For some time, I noticed that we were getting an increased number of calls from groups asking if the authors were available to speak at luncheons, meetings, or special events. Based on these requests, I thought of a way to capitalize on the requests by suggesting to my bosses that it would be a good idea for the company to start a speakers bureau. It would gain exposure not only for the company but also for the authors and would be an additional forum for selling books."

Her bosses told her that they liked the idea but couldn't see a way to make it happen or how to fund it. They decided not to undertake the venture.

"One evening, shortly afterward, I was having a drink with a colleague and happened to tell her about my speaker bureau plan and the company's response. She also thought it was a great idea because it combined a number of my interests, experiences, and skills. Soon I forgot about it, and life in publishing went on."

Some time later, the company downsized, eliminating Arlynn's job. She happened to be meeting with the same friend, and they discussed Arlynn's options. "My friend reminded me of the speakers bureau idea and said it was the perfect business for me to start. But the thought of starting my own business after 20 years in my field was uncomfortable. So I decided to cushion the impact by proposing a speakers bureau for the AAP [Association of American Publishers]. I was told to write a proposal, develop a strategic plan, and create a financial projection. I then had to make the presentation to the heads of all the member publishing houses, and that was just nerve-racking. After I finished, they asked me to leave the room so they could vote on my proposal. It felt like high school, but with a lot more at stake. They thought I had a gem of an idea and proposal and suggested that I do the speakers bureau. They said that they would be supportive.

"Their comments gave me the confidence and impetus I needed. As I already had done the work and research, I tweaked the proposal into a business plan and included the strategic plan and financial projection. I knew that my niche focus would be placing authors in speaking engagements. To be sure it would cause no future problems with my former employers, I discussed my plan with them, and they gave me the all clear."

Arlynn Greenbaum created Authors Unlimited, a successful specialty speakers bureau that books over 150 engagements a year for such literary luminaries as Anita Shreve, Walter Isaacson, Judith Viorst, Anne Perry, and Simon Winchester (as well as yours truly). Arlynn Greenbaum is on the board of International Association of Speakers Bureaus and remains connected to the world of books and publishing. She successfully made lemonade from that lemon of a layoff.

———————————————■———————————————

Points to Ponder

What did Arlynn do that helped her create a business out
of a layoff?

- She **listened** to the marketplace and remembered the
  volume of requests she had received at the publishing
  house for guest speakers who had written books.
- She had an idea and thoroughly **researched** it to
  assess whether there was a need and a paying market for a speakers bureau of authors.
- She did the **due diligence:** She developed a proposal,
  a strategic plan, and financial projections that would
  form the basis of a business plan.
- Even before needing job change advice, she **built
  friendships** with colleagues in the industry with
  whom she could share her idea.

———————————————■———————————————

When it came time to solicit support and job ideas,
Arlynn's network was in place. This was a **preneed network,** which according to John Hull of Intel Capital, is
essential for people in the workplace. Within this network
of friends that Arlynn had made was one who listened to
her, remembered her creative proposal, and, most of all,
encouraged her. Arlynn also made sure to clear her idea
with her former boss in order to avoid subsequent problems. Although many people would not have bothered to
do this, Arlynn preferred to keep things on the up and
up—it's called integrity.

One of the most important lessons we can learn from
Arlynn Greenbaum's decision to scrap her job search,
which might only have resulted in another layoff, and

take the risk to start her business is to be active in your industry and community and maintain friendships. Arlynn established a preneed network consisting of resources and people to offer support and advice. Anyone contemplating a similar decision would be wise to follow her example. Don't just join the professional organizations associated with your field. Become involved and sign up for a committee to develop visibility and connections to colleagues. Nurture those relationships with phone calls, notes or e-mail, and an occasional cup of coffee (or beverage of your choice). Offer help to others and request it for yourself when you need it.

"BABY" BLUES BROTHER

These days, a computer crash can be as disastrous as a stock market crash. We are so computer dependent that a day without one can cause the CTs (computer tremens). This happened to my "baby" brother and almost made him sing the blues.

One day I called and asked him how he was doing. Ira answered, "I'm great. This has been the best week I have had in the business since Dad died." My brother and Dad were in business together for two decades as Rosenberg Paper Brokers, but Dad had been in the paper biz for 60 years.

Of course, I was curious. What could possibly have happened to make this week such a great one? And could we bottle it?

"Oh, that's an easy answer," Ira responded. "The quick version is that my computer died."

"Oh?" I asked. That really didn't sound like good news.

Ira continued, "Normally I get to work, log on, answer e-mail, someone IMs [instant messages] me, and we get into conversation. Then I have to check my Rotisserie

League and Fantasy team results and go to ESPN.com and check out scores. It's a busy morning.

"Without my computer, I just stared at the hole in the office and had nothing to do. So I went back to my Rolodex and started to call some of my old customers and some of my former customers. They all know I am the long-standing Cubs fan and a Bulls fan, so we would chat about trades, the season; we talked about our kids and our parents, and so on. Almost to a one, they each gave me an order. Whoa! This 'no computer' thing wasn't so bad. And it was going to be in the shop for a week.

"I made plans to make a couple of sales calls. Once I was in Joliet for one guy, I realized I was almost in the neighborhood for a couple of other longtime customers in nearby towns. Each visit and conversation turned into another order. A couple of visits turned into two orders. Of course, being away from my morning office routine was frustrating, but my sales figures were off the charts."

Ira's bad experience forced him to develop new routines. Change can often be disconcerting, but when forced to do so, we may stumble into better business practices, as Ira did. What might have sent this small business and its owner into a tailspin ended up enabling him to spin straw into sales-figure gold. But the real issue is what Ira learned and what he changed as a result.

Ira explains, "Now that the computer is where it should be, I still check my e-mail, my different leagues, but I make sure that I continue to pick up the phone more often and talk to my customers with more regularity. And I make sure I schedule sales calls so I get to shake hands with my customers more often. Then when I go home, I check the rest of my scores and ESPN after work."

Applying the personal touch, having a real-time conversation with his customers, and taking pains to visit them face-to-face turned a computer failure into a sales success for Ira. That was some sweet and lucrative lemonade that he squeezed out of his computer lemon.

Current economic factors in the job market are forcing people to reassess their work situations. Taking a stop-gap job or a temporary one is not something they want to do, but they do it and make something more than they had anticipated out of it.

TYPING HIS WAY TO SUCCESS

Chuck Montgomery taught chorus, piano, and choir in the San Francisco public high schools. He was the devoted accompanist and director of an outstanding and award-winning gospel choir that performed at many civic functions. After a number of years, the stresses and the pace required by these responsibilities prompted him to take a leave of absence. As a result of the agility he developed from his years of playing the piano, he could type over 100 words a minute, so he signed up with a temporary employment agency.

Chuck spoke on a panel at one of the career change seminars I offered for teachers in 1980. As a successfully transitioned former teacher, he explained that one of his first positions after teaching was with a division of Bank of America . . . as a typist. "The managers would give me their reports and I would quickly type them," he explained. "While they did appreciate my speed and quick turnaround, they began to notice that, once typed, their reports read better than the draft. Sentences were well crafted and flowed in an organized pattern. The punctuation was perfect and every word was correctly spelled. [Author's comment: This was the pre-spell-check era, but relying on spell-check is a big mistake in any case].

Finally, one of the managers mentioned these transformations to me and asked me about my background. When I told him that I have a master's degree in English from Ole Miss, my job changed. I was offered a permanent position." Rather than merely tell the managers and executives at the bank that the department needed the expertise of the English major to make reports read well, Chuck had shown them.

At the workshop, one teacher who was facing a layoff asked Chuck whether he missed his work with the students and his choir. "Not yet," he replied, "but I know that if I do, I can volunteer my time and let my music be my avocation. There are plenty of opportunities for volunteers in our schools and community."

Despite the sea of finance, accounting, and MBA degrees that might have drained him, Chuck's liberal arts degree paid off. He also was an avid reader of several local and national newspapers. He often noticed various articles that focused on recurring themes. When the theme was of interest to or seemed to indicate the beginning of a trend that might impact banking, financial services consumers, and allied industries, he would mention his observations in formal meetings and casually at the watercooler. An executive again took notice of his expertise, and a position as a trend spotter was created for him to do just that.

"I can't believe I get paid to do what I love doing . . . and was doing anyway," Chuck enthused at the career seminar. Eventually, he was made a vice president at Bank of America, where he remained for the rest of his life.

Job burnout affects many of us. We develop a sort of tunnel vision, seeing only what we already do, which sometimes obscures what we **could** do if necessary. Chuck sought a temporary job as a typist, acknowledging a part of his skills base that had not been his main career focus. As a result of his hard work, experience, talents, and insights, he turned it into a career that he loved. He did not enter the typing pool complaining that his master's degree in English made him overqualified; he simply applied his skills and made the writing of others look good. By remaining open to the possibilities, Chuck was able to parlay the observations and conclusions he gleaned from his reading into a successful career change that was truly music to his ears.

The events that take place in some people's lives are neither what they expected nor what they planned, and there is a measure of pain involved. The resulting scar can be permanent, yet others find a way to heal themselves and minimize the damage.

BLESSINGS IN DISGUISE

Desiree Daniels believes that everything happens for a reason. She has had searing firsthand experience of the "six degrees of separation" phenomenon, which could have broken her spirit, but she found a way to rise above it. "When I was younger and would be disappointed about something," Desiree begins, "my mother used to tell me, 'Desiree, this very well may be a blessing in disguise.' Until I moved to Japan in August of 2000, I never really understood what she meant."

She continues, "In March 2000, my boyfriend suggested that we move to Japan for a year. Chris said that we could teach at the English Conversation School where his sister worked. I decided it would be a good experience. He left two months before me. We had our teaching contracts, jobs, and residency all lined up. I stayed in Canada to finish my job at the bank (which I hated) and to prepare for my upcoming year living abroad. I remember feeling anxious on the flight. I was flooded with a mix of emotions and fears: of a new culture, a new career, and experiencing the unknown, as well as the excitement of being reunited with Chris. I was also ready for the challenge of taking our relationship to the next level.

"When I arrived on a Thursday night, something was different. Chris was not making eye contact with me. His first words when he saw me were, 'Hey . . . you look sunburnt.' I knew at that exact moment that life was going to take a drastic change of direction. That next morning he said that he wanted us to break up.

"Various thoughts and words came to mind, and most of them were not very nice, but I heard a voice that was louder and more powerful. It sounded like my grandma telling me, 'Desiree, you did not come here for him, so don't miss out on this.' She inspired me to make a decision.

"I told Chris that I wasn't leaving and if that was uncomfortable for him, then he could leave. He didn't leave. He stayed, and so did I. This meant a commitment of eight months, working and living in the same space. I decided at that very moment that I was going to make my life in Japan about me. **I was going to take every opportunity, every invitation, and every possibility.** I would re-create my life in Japan as an independent woman, starting a new journey of self-discovery. It was as if a new me had emerged, and I could take on the world.

"Give me a lemon and I will make lemonade. I was pretty good at that, although at this point, I felt like I had been given a box of dried-out lemons with no juice left to squeeze. I turned my attention to the world around me— in particular, the job that prompted my move across the ocean. In my various classes, I observed each of my students, and it became clear to me that I wanted to know about these people who were my students: their dreams, their lives, and their stories. It was a risk because privacy was part of the Japanese culture. Because I wanted to ask questions that really mattered, I took the plunge and asked only those things that were important.

"My students, ages 20 to 70, in groups of five or six or one on one, started telling me about their lives. They were flower buds . . . just waiting to be opened and begin to blossom. And they did.

"That is how it started. I worked with these women and so many more, listening to their experiences, challenging them on their ideas, exploring their visions and dreams. I used the knowledge I had as a psychology graduate to guide them to where they needed to go. I loved it! Whether we met in coffee shops or classrooms, it didn't matter. My mission was to help these women realize their goals. As I watched them blossom, I wondered if I could do this in Canada.

"My boss, Mieko, was a 52-year-old, single Japanese mother who created the English Conversation School. She started tutoring English to young adults in her home to support her son. Soon it grew into groups of students, and then, to meet the demand, she opened a school. Twenty years later, with three English Conversation Schools, located in Osaka, Nagoya, and Tokyo, Mieko inspired me to dream of having my own business."

After Desiree had made this decision, she returned to Vancouver and started telling her plans to everyone she knew—and asked them to tell everyone *they* knew. Serendipity happens at interesting junctures in time. As Desiree remembers, "My dad said to me, 'Des, when it's right, it all falls into place.' The very next day, my best friend's mom showed me an article on a new field called 'personal coaching' and said, 'Des, I think this sounds close to what you say you want to do, and I think you would be good at it.' She referred me to a coach she knew of in Vancouver.

"I hired my own coach and started experiencing the

profession firsthand. Within a week of our sessions, my coach referred me to a coaching and counseling college. I began training there, as well as working at the college as a student advisor. A year later, after graduation, I launched my own business in the personal development field.

"It's been almost three years since landing in Japan on that humid night in August. I am in the middle of building my company, Simple Life Solutions. As I become more integrated in the business community and develop connections with so many amazing individuals, I realize that opportunity is everywhere, and it's our choice whether or not we embrace it.

"What seemed like a nightmare became a blessing in disguise because, as Dad said, when everything is right, things fall into place."

Desiree listened to her gut, followed her interests, corralled her courage, and seized the opportunity she had. She is now teaching others how to find the strength, desire, and attitude to do the same.

ACTING SCHOOLS

At times, even seemingly perfect plans go awry, and we must be ready to respond. The career of your dreams doesn't always pan out—at least not immediately. When John Goodman appeared on *Inside the Actors Studio* (one of my favorite shows), he was asked by a graduating third-year acting student, "What would you recommend that we [graduating students] do?" Goodman immediately answered, "Learn to type." Then he explained that actors need a skill that will put food on the table while they are waiting for the big break. Some actors type, others wait tables, and still others find that substitute teaching fills the bill.

Substitute teaching seemed like the perfect use of Alan Simon's degree in English. "I was an actor by night, and by day . . . a per diem substitute in the New York City schools and that was a difficult job that wasn't satisfactory," he says. "Some people think that the acting training may help the substitute teacher because each has an audience that must be engaged. That's not true. Theater audiences **want** to be entertained. Not so a class whose teacher is out sick. But being an actor is tough, and I was far too overextended. I had just placed my mother in a nursing home, and it was a hard thing to do. Then in 1982 a friend called—an actor-producer type who knew that I also taught. She reminded me that the Screen Actors Guild basic agreement had changed and now allowed for on-site education of minors in the profession. She mentioned that she and another mutual friend both thought I would be perfect because of my dual careers.

"The idea intrigued me and was the perfect melding of my acting and my teacher skills and networks in both arenas. I took the time to investigate the agreement, what it entailed, the issues of implementation and licensing, and On Location Education was born. I taught the students in television series, films, and on Broadway. For me, it was a way to be part of show business rather than just being an actor. It was the best of both of my worlds.

"One season we received the contracts for *Kate & Allie* and *The Cosby Show*, which were both shot in New York. It was my big break as well. I had to hire several other teachers to work for me. Of course, I hired people I knew to be really good teachers. Then companies I had previously worked with that were going on the road wanted me to arrange for teachers. One was going on tour to D.C. and another to Orlando, and I had to find the best teachers for the young actors. And I did. My business then became a national business. We not only check out teachers for their educational experience, we look at their entire background, get references, and make sure they are the right fit for the students.

"Subsequently, I have become involved in an advocacy role for child actors and sit on several committees in Screen Actors Guild and Actors' Equity. Once I started my business, I learned more about the many careers that are available in the business. So being an educator, I designed alternative career seminars because some of the young actors had no clue what an A.D. [assistant director] or a stage manager or a producer does. They need to know the other options in show business that they could pursue.

"Those seminars gave me back my chops and brought me back to performance. I began to think of what I really wanted to do—for me—and realized that it was cabaret. When I left show business I was doing a one-man show, and in two months I will premiere my one-man show in Manhattan. My overlapping careers really have come full circle."

Alan Simon took two careers that weren't making their mark, each with its own set of problems, and turned them into a business that combines his talents and serves the best of both worlds. Although you might dismiss it as sheer luck that he received that initial call from his friend, there is more than that involved.

First, Alan was **open** about his day job and did not keep the other part of his life private. He let his actor pals know that he also worked as a teacher and that substitute teaching was tough. He had colleagues in both fields, so he had a network of acquaintances and coworkers and kept in touch with them. Second, when Alan received that intriguing call about the new SAG regulations, he *heard* the message. The timing was right; he **took action** and DID the *due diligence* it takes to investigate, research, and then launch a new business that would meet the necessary standards and regulations. Finally, as a former teacher, I can tell you that everyday Alan met with his students, whether before, in between, or after performances, he had **prepared** those lesson plans to ensure his students were getting the best possible education. And he hires other teachers who do the same. In this way, he developed such a solid reputation for himself that his services are in demand and his business gets positive word of mouth.

THE ART OF LIVING

Many people do things in their daily lives that turn the difficult experiences they have into something worthwhile. If you have visited the self-help section of any bookstore, you have seen how many books are testimonies to life situations that could have gone south but were transformed into something positive. Writers share their personal experiences through various formats— whether as blogs (web logs), articles in the community paper, or entries in a personal journal. An exasperated father of two teenage daughters, a sportswriter by trade, started talking about his experiences at work and was encouraged to write them up as columns for the paper. Those columns were later collected in one of the most sidesplittingly hilarious books I have ever read: *8 Simple Rules for Dating My Teenage Daughter,* by W. Bruce Cameron, which was the basis for the television show of the same name.

Although writing is not the right outlet for everyone, it's one way to deal with a bad hand. Keeping a journal can be therapeutic, and that makes the effort a good investment. Journal entries can serve as sources of material for short stories, essays, articles, plans, and even books. Comedians are well known for using their life experiences as the foundation for their shtick. Ray Romano's twin sons and family life are themes for his situation comedy, *Everybody Loves Raymond*, as are Bernie Mac's experiences of raising his sister's three children.

Music is yet another way to express the pain of life's situations. Listen to the words of some popular songs, and you will recognize themes that are very personal. The blues emerged from hard times and life experiences that were challenging and downright tough, resulting in a genre of music whose current sovereign is B.B. King.

Some people tell their stories through dance or poetry or visual arts. Movie houses and the stage, from Broadway to community theater, bring to life the experiences of playwrights and screenwriters. Exploring galleries and museums likewise reveals the results of how some creative people cope with life situations.

There are also less public ways of expressing a life. A colleague of mine, an engineer who assesses fatal work-related accidents, spends his leisure time creating magnificent pieces of furniture from wood. Several people I know are gardeners. One of my most senior friends, who was 87 years old and lived alone, bred roses and was a member of the local rose club. She found that planting, weeding, and tending her garden allowed her to continue to create and nurture life. An added bonus was the beauty of the roses in her life and those of us lucky enough to share it with her.

Some days, just talking about difficult life situations seems to improve them.

TELL ME A STORY

We all know someone who has a remarkable history or personal story. Some people have the gift of telling their stories well and making them come alive. Actor Peter Coyote, who has made more than 90 movies and was once head of the California Arts Council, is one of those people. The Mill Valley Film Festival sponsored a tribute to him, at which I heard him speak. His stories were interesting, but it was the way he told them that captivated the audience. Some of his stories described occurrences that had not been pleasant at the time, but as so often happens, they get funnier in the retelling. The old adage says that humor is tragedy plus time. Steve Allen frequently gets credit for that nugget, but it is actually from the Talmud, which has been around for centuries. The ability to transform an unfortunate situation into a funny anecdote is a very attractive trait. We can learn from those who add time to their tribulation, creating from them personal and professional stories that come alive, capture our attention, and invite us to laugh with them. Turning a bad time into a last laugh is even better than making lemonade.

These are some of the people whose You Never Know! experiences prompted them to make the best of a bad situation. They behaved optimistically even if, at that time, they weren't feeling so positive. They capitalized on their crisis by taking action, avoiding being immobilized by seemingly insurmountable obstacles. They assessed risks, made decisions, rose to the occasion, and behaved admirably. In some cases, they researched new professions and creative options, did the due diligence, and, most of all, stayed *open to the possibility* without getting bogged down in the probability. They listened to the market, heeded their own gut-level reactions, acted on opportunities, powered through tough times, and turned those lemons into the lemonade of success. If they can do it, so can we.

---■---

RoAne's Reminders

The You Never Know It Alls in this chapter experienced an event that did not seem favorable at the time. All of them not only got through it, but managed to turn it around into something positive.

To turn lemons into lemonade

- **Seek** out the positive—look for the silver lining in the clouds.
- **Establish** a network of support and maintain it.
- **Ask** difficult questions as part of a self-assessment.
- **Observe** role models both for what they do and for what they say.
- **Pay attention** to your gut and to the marketplace.
- **Accept compliments.**
- **Take seriously** ideas that pop into your head.
- **Write** these ideas down.
- **Laugh** at yourself.
- **Pick up the phone** and connect to someone in real time.
- **Have a plan.**
- ***Work hard!***

---■---

Furthermore, each one of these lemonade makers exhibited at least one of the eight counterintuitive traits that helped turn their negative into a positive. When unpleasant circumstances catch You Never Know It Alls off guard, they stay *open* and motivate themselves to find solutions.

Lemonade Anyone? An Action Plan

Each person you've just read about took a bad situation and made it work. *How* did these people take their sour lemons and turn them into lemonade, and what can you learn from each of them?

	What did each person do?	**What can you borrow from each?**
Ira	_____	_____
Arlynn	_____	_____
Chuck	_____	_____
Desiree	_____	_____
Alan	_____	_____

The success of the people profiled in this chapter was born of the actions they took based on reactions they had to a situation that was sour. Their successes were not the work of magic, nor did they result from plain dumb luck. They did their homework, they made considered choices, and they worked with what they were dealt. That made all the difference.

IT'S A SMALL WORLD

My favorite line from *When Harry Met Sally* had nothing to do with Meg Ryan's scene in the deli. For me, the most memorable line was Billy Crystal's comment in the furniture store, delivered with his trademark punch: Of course he would run into his ex-wife in *that* furniture store in New York, a city of eight million people. It represents the consummate "small world" story, in which we bump into someone we know in an unexpected place—but might have preferred not to.

There are several variations on this "small world" theme:

- We bump into people we know in a likely place and are happy to see them.
- We bump into people we know and are happy to see them, but it's in an unlikely place.
- We meet someone we don't know in an unlikely place, but find out that we know people in common, and a connection is made.

The lives of those who seek serendipity and embrace it are a series of such coincidences and experiences. These people discover the pattern through conversations that establish common acquaintances and connect the dots of their daily lives. When I was growing up in Chicago, home of what I call the "Concord Grapevine," we always wanted to know whether people we met knew people we knew, because that made the world smaller and brought us closer together.

Friendster.com, which now has more than 2 million users, has built a business based on an expansion of the idea that whoever I know includes whoever you know and whoever they know, and so on. It's like a Ponzi scheme based on acquaintances, friends, and potential new friends and contacts. Your Friendster friends' names are downloaded, much like MP3 files. In an issue of *Fortune* magazine, David Kirkpatrick writes, "There are over 15 social-networking companies that build links with built-in references. These numbers of companies and users will increase because we have a generation that uses their computers and the Internet to communicate, research, shop and chat."[1] There are currently over 30 dot-com businesses, including Linked In, many of which are supported by venture capital funds, and we can thus assume that those who need help amassing a network of contacts through online services constitute a growing demographic. Who we know and how many people we know is important these days.

The creation of social networks, whether in person or online, is based on our need for community and connection—shared experiences, shared wants, and shared people. "Knowing people in common takes the big world and gives it a smaller, more manageable context," according to Vannessa Hua of the *San Francisco Chronicle*. Why is this so important? Because of the venerable law of success that states: It's not what you know but *whom* you know. In *The Secrets of Savvy Networking* (Warner Books,

NON SEQUITUR © 2003 Wiley Miller. Dist.
By UNIVERSAL PRESS SYNDICATE.

1993), I took this up a notch by adding a pearl from my "femtor," (female mentor) Sally Livingston: **"It is who knows *you*."** Our contacts and connections contribute to our lives just as we do to theirs. The successful results of "small world" experiences can impact both our bottom line and the quality of our life.

These days many people meet online, but we all meet people under a variety of circumstances. When we discover that they know someone we know (or ought to know), do what we do, or have been where we've been, our response is (with a bow to Mr. Disney), "It's a small world after all." This explains what seems to be coincidental, the result of kismet or destiny, or simply what's "meant to be." Both my professional and my personal life have been enriched and made more joyful and fun because of this "small world" of wonderful coincidences.

It's a special delight to meet someone in a faraway place and discover that we know someone in common.

DOWN UNDER

As the result of just such a successful "do you know who I know?" conversation, I missed Thanksgiving in 1993. I didn't really miss it—I just wasn't *here* for it.

Patricia Fripp, British-born and San Francisco–based professional speaker and coach, was in Australia giving several programs. When she finished, Diane, a member of the audience who owns a media and advertising firm in Australia, approached her and said that one of her favorite business authors lived in San Francisco. "She wondered if there was a possibility that I might know her," Patricia said. "Because I am very practical, I explained that San Francisco is a city with over 750,000 inhabitants and that made the chances very slim. But out of curiosity, I asked her who it was. When she said that it was 'Susan RoAne who wrote *How to Work a Room,* I looked at her in amazement. 'You aren't going to believe this, but not only do I know her . . . she is one of my best friends!' I suggested Diane give me her card and said that I would give it to Susan RoAne and that she could expect a call."

When Patricia returned, she called and told me of this very small world coincidence, said she was mailing the card, and suggested that I get in touch with Diane and offer to do some programs in Australia. I know great advice when I hear it! I faxed first, and then called Diane, and we discussed the need for workshops in several cities in Australia. And that's why in November 1993 I missed Thanksgiving—because I was teaching the strategies for working a room in a lovely room in beautiful Sydney, Australia.

How did this "small world" connection turn into a successful business venture? All three of us took actions that turned Diane's original question about whom Patricia knew in San Francisco into a series of seminars serving the business communities of three cities in Australia.

Points to Ponder

Diane did several things to make this "small world" event happen. She signed up for Patricia's program and read the biography, which told her that Patricia was also from San Francisco. She summoned her courage and curiosity to ask the speaker a personal question that might have been considered a real long shot. When she did hear from me, she responded to my initial message and followed through to plan a series of presentations in Australia. Diane did a lot of work to make this happen:

- She assessed the market and the level of interest.
- She explored strategic partnerships for investment.
- She worked her media leads to ensure publicity.
- She lined up venues and planned menus.
- She developed a marketing plan with a PR budget.
- She arranged for the registration process.
- She organized my Australia tour.

Patricia Fripp played a large part in this "small world" story because she took the initiative to make the connection. She offered to take Diane's card back to the United States, mailed it to me, and called me to be sure I followed up with the seminar series.

What did I do to make this "small world" story add Australia to my world travels? I followed Patricia's advice and called Australia, brainstorming with Diane to make the series of three seminars in Australia a reality.

The chance that a speaker from San Francisco knew a San Francisco–based author was good but by no means guaranteed. The chance that we would be best of friends was very slim! Diane might have opted to not even ask the question because she thought the odds of Patricia knowing me were too minuscule to risk sounding foolish. Nevertheless, she took a chance. As Chapter 1 told us, one of the eight traits of You Never Know It Alls is that they "drop names" of people they know, places they have lived, and schools they have attended in order to make connections. They seize the opportunities to identify common ground. Regardless of whether you actually turn out to know people in common, the bottom line is that you might connect with a potential contact, associate, or friend.

A recent study by noted British psychologist Dr. Richard Wiseman, reported in *Psychology Today,* found that people who consider themselves fortunate cultivate larger networks than other people.[3] These networks can be farther-reaching than we think, if we are confident enough to tap into them. The play *Six Degrees of Separation,* in which a young man claims to be actor Sydney Poitier's son in order to establish connections, popularized the concept of a small world of connections. To be precise, though, the research of Stanley Milgram indicates that there are actually 5.5 degrees mathematically separating people, according to *Linked* (Perseus, 2002), by Dr. Albert-Laszlo Barabasi, a physicist at the University of Notre Dame. However, playwright John Guare knew that *Six Degrees of Separation* was alliterative, as well as a more memorable and punchier title. More important, Milgram's findings demonstrate that "small world" experiences are abundant and available to all of us. Just think about the "small world" events in your own life. We often discount things we do ourselves to contribute to a positive outcome, failing to give ourselves credit for our own actions and responses. To increase our opportunities, it's worth taking a closer look at our own behavior.

Your "Small World" Event (Who, What, When, and Where)	What You Did and Said	The Result
1. _____	_____	_____
2. _____	_____	_____
3. _____	_____	_____
4. _____	_____	_____
5. _____	_____	_____

AFTER-HOURS CALL

In some cases, separation is only two degrees, as it was for Shirley Davalos, media coach and trainer. According to Shirley, "It was a Friday night about 6:30 P.M., and I was just about to leave the office to go home after a very long week, when the phone rang. My daughters were little and I wanted to get home, but I answered it anyway. I could tell by the voice it was a very elderly man. He said his daughter wanted to produce an exercise video and that he was gathering information. When he said that his daughter lived in Santa Cruz, it was clear he wasn't a potential client. But I just spent 10 minutes or so on the phone with him giving him ideas and suggestions. To me, it was sweet that he wanted to help his daughter.

"Six weeks later I had to give a presentation for a San Francisco–based corporation that wanted to produce a video. The presentation went well, but the team leader explained that they were waiting for Joe, the archivist, who had the final say. We could hear him coming down the hallway, as he had two canes that clicked on the tile. The team leader filled Joe in on my presentation and we chatted a bit. I gave Joe my card. He looked at me and said, 'Shirley Davalos of Orion Express, I know you.'

"I had no idea how he knew me. But then he explained that late one Friday, he had found my name in a phone book and spoke to me about his daughter's exercise video. He told me that I was very nice and helpful to him."

As you would expect, Shirley was on the short list for the video project. There's no question that answering Joe's call was inconvenient. Taking the time to talk to him and provide helpful information was likewise inconvenient. But Shirley Davalos is gracious.

There is no way Shirley ever thought she would hear from the elderly gentleman again, much less meet him. It's a small world indeed when the person you take a few moments to help turns out to be the archivist who has the final say on a contract for your business.

Because it is a small world, it pays to be nice to everyone.

Sometimes our past and present lives converge in a totally unexpected way.

THE JESUIT JAZZ CONNECTION

Father Frank Coco, is a Jesuit priest and former teacher at Jesuit High in New Orleans. Father Frank also plays jazz clarinet, jamming in local clubs such as Pete Fountain's famous venue. He has a following of jazz buffs, as well as students, parishioners, and fellow priests who are fans of his "other" path. He combined both of his callings on his CD, *An Evening of Jesuit Jazz*. Thanks to a "small world" incident, Father Frank has just reconnected with Father Joe Eagan, his fellow seminarian from five decades ago at St. Mary's in Kansas.

Here's how it happened. Father Joe is associate pastor at St. Patrick's Church in Larkspur, California. Church member Sandy Hufford was reading her issue of *New Orleans* magazine, where she saw an article about Father Frank. Since Father Joe was celebrating his fiftieth year as a Jesuit priest, Sandy thought Father Frank's CD would be the perfect gift to give him.

Rather than just ordering the CD, Sandy, the consummate networker, took the time to send a note explaining that she had read the article about Father Frank and that the CD was intended as a gift for Father Joe, a fellow Jesuit. "When I received the CD," Sandy says, "it was accompanied by a lovely note from Father Frank saying that this was an 'amazing coincidence.'" The note explained that Father Frank knew Father Joe but had lost track of him. In fact, they were old friends who had gone to seminary together. He inscribed the CD as a gift from an old friend—a true treasure.

"When I gave Father Joe the gift, his face lit right up!" Sandy continues. "He had many memories of visits to

New Orleans for conferences, where he would often go with Father Frank to Pete Fountain's performances in the French Quarter and meet jazz greats who would drop in to see Pete between shows."

It is indeed a small world. You never know how large an impact a small gift might have. Two old friends reconnect because of a parishioner's serendipitous networking—as though it had been ordained to happen.

Occasionally it turns out that the stranger seated next to us *does* know someone we know.

GULFPORT PEOPLE

Following a luncheon speech to the International Association of Convention and Visitors Bureaus, I was seated at a table with some of the members. We had introduced ourselves and started to chat. When I read my luncheon partner's name tag and saw that it said Gulfport, Mississippi, that was all I needed. But first I took a deep breath and said, "Stephen, I only know *one* person in all of Gulfport, so this is going to be a really odd question. Do you happen to know John 'Shorty' Sneed?" Stephen Richer gave me the strangest look. After what seemed like a very long pause he said, "Of course I do! He's the bureau's insurance agent. How do you know him?" I told him that we had met on a plane years ago and had stayed in touch. I asked if he had heard what happened to Shorty's daughter, Lori, who had just been severely injured by a drunk driver. Our conversation was no longer just small talk. Once we discovered our connection, we began to discuss Shorty, Lori, and the situation.

What if Stephen hadn't known my buddy? My question still might have opened up lines of communication. He may have asked me what my friend does or if I had ever been to Gulfport to visit the family. I could have said a few words about how I met Shorty and then asked Stephen about Gulfport. As unlikely as it might have been, my original question did lead to a more interesting conversation. As is sometimes the case, this You Never Know! opportunity turned out to be a "you never know who someone also knows" scenario, and that makes for a "very small world" connection.

As a direct result of that conversation after my speech, Stephen recommended me to another group that hired me to speak. If I had said nothing about my Gulfport friend, we might not have initiated the conversation and developed the rapport that motivated Stephen to recommend me. That connection was solid, because we still keep in touch.

I can now look back at the event and identify which of the eight traits were in play:

1. I talked to a stranger. Of course, I had just finished giving the luncheon keynote speech to 500 convention and bureau professionals on the topic of how to work a room. Shame on me if I didn't talk to the person I didn't know sitting to my left.

2. I dropped a name. Although I knew I sounded foolish, I wanted to know whether, with all those people living in Gulfport, Stephen knew Shorty. Dropping the names of people, places, movies or books is how we start the process of learning who or what we have in common in this "small world."

3. We never considered our conversation about Lori's accident to be small talk, but we also never talked about current affairs, the economics of the convention industry, or the impact of bond issues on the funding of convention centers. All of these topics might have qualified as Big Talk. Our conversation

about Lori, the accident, and the Sneed family may have been "small" by comparison, but it was big enough for us.

Postscript

Stephen Richer and I still are in touch, as I am with Shorty Sneed. Shorty and his wife, Patti, and I recently had dinner in New Orleans—almost 20 years after we first met on a plane.

NAILING THE DEAL

The alumnae of Syracuse University will soon have something besides their alma mater in common: They will have their very own color of nail polish, created for them by Essie Cosmetics. Of course, we expect that such a marketing decision would have been made in a strategic planning session, at a board meeting, or during a powwow with the development director of the university. Not in this book. This decision was made in the unscientific, unplanned, coincidental manner resulting from a chance meeting and the ensuing small talk between two strangers that took place in the very "small world" on an elevator in a Park Avenue building in New York City.

Lauren Oberman was just leaving a meeting in one of the apartments in a building on Park Avenue and 75th Street. "I was in the elevator when a woman and man got in, and she looked at my hands and asked me what was the color of my nail polish," explains Lauren. "I told her it was 'Adore-a-Ball.' She said, 'Very nice!' and then asked what color my toenail polish was, and I told her it was 'Fishnet Stockings.' She said, 'Perfect,' and then asked what brand. When I said it was Essie, she said, 'Oh, that's my favorite!' I told her that I agreed and added that

I sometimes use 'Ballet Slippers.' She said that was her favorite color and was wearing it then. While our conversation made the elevator ride go very fast, I thought it was odd that some random woman was asking me all these questions about nail polish. Hey, it's New York City and anything is possible, right?

"I was curious and looked on www.essie.com and found a page about the founder and, lo and behold, there is a photo of Essie Weingarten, founder and president of Essie Cosmetics. Of course, it was the woman in the elevator. She started her successful business in 1981 and designed her own signature square bottle. She not only has the best nail polish colors, they have the coolest names, too.

"I sent an e-mail to the 'contact us' section that basically said how funny it was that I met her in an elevator, etc. Well, she wrote me back and said this:

Dear Lauren,

It was my pleasure meeting you, however, I really never introduce myself because I love to hear the real comments from consumers. Of course, if they know it's me then I only hear all the good stuff. However, it usually does not happen in our building. Needless to say, I never saw you before so it was as candid as it gets.

Thanks again.

Essie

"I wrote her back that night and attached my 'signature' with my work information. The phone rang the next morning and I picked it up and heard, 'Hi Lauren, it's Essie.'

"I never expected to hear from her and was thrilled. We chatted, and she laughed and said she 'was so embarrassed that I figured her out.' When she saw that (at that time) I worked at *Shape* magazine, she said she had been working with our beauty editor on promoting her summer colors all summer!

"When she asked why I was in her building in the first place, I told her that I was part of a Syracuse alumni mentoring group that mentors high school students, and we're having a tenth anniversary celebration in September, with 600 people including students. I was addressing and stuffing invites in someone's apartment that night in her building. *Then* she actually offered to create a Syracuse color nail polish for the event and donate it to the students.

"Needless to say, I was quite excited and so was our leader, who lives in her building. She will, no doubt, be calling Essie to invite her to the event and ask if she'd create the Syracuse nail polish for the entire university!

"Essie ended up creating a special name for our tenth anniversary event: 'Decade of Friends' because the group is called the Friends of Leadership—'Leadership' being the High School for Leadership and Public Service. She donated about 300 bottles or more of the polish."

You never know where a bit of small talk with a stranger might lead. Had Essie not talked to the young woman wearing one of her nail polishes and had Lauren not graciously responded, mentioning her favorite color, or followed through on her curiosity and instincts, she would never have learned that she was speaking with Essie herself. And the Friends of Leadership would not have their signature polish to benefit the students at the High School for Leadership and Public Service.

Because boundaries between business and personal lives are frequently blurred, calling to hire someone's professional services—and being open to serendipity—can allow for an outcome that can change our lives.

A VERY SMALL WORLD: HEIDI'S STORY

When Heidi Rodino learned that her third child, Jacob, was aphasic, it seemed as if her world was crashing around her. Her infant son, Andrew, had also been diagnosed with a retino blastoma (a rare cancer of the eye), and the doctors were planning surgery to remove the eye. And yet she still had to make arrangements for Jacob's therapy.

"When I was given the name of a speech therapist, I had to call her," Heidi remembers. "We discussed his condition and her recommendation, but I felt I had to be honest about my situation. I told her that if I seemed somewhat distant and distracted that I wasn't ignoring Jacob's therapy. It made sense to tell her about Andrew's condition and his impending surgery. She asked the name of his doctor and that surprised me, but I told her. Her response sent chills down my back. She said that her son had the exact same condition, the same doctors, and the same operation that Andrew faced."

When the speech therapist mentioned that her son had worn a glass eye for several years, the conversation took a different turn because of their common bond. Heidi explained that she was concerned about her other children and their adjustment to Andrew's situation.

Heidi goes on, "Then this woman—who minutes before was a stranger who I was hiring as a speech therapist—became an angel. She offered to come over with her son to show my children how normal he is and have him show them the removable eye so they would be prepared for Andrew's return. What she did for me by sharing her son's situation gave me comfort, hope, and solace. I am forever grateful to her."

The speech therapist has a private practice based on

billable hours. She could have kept her son's condition to herself and responded to this potential client in the predictable fashion. She did not have to volunteer to visit. Her generous offer to familiarize Heidi's other children and help them adjust to their brother's condition was unexpected and treasured by Heidi.

Of all the speech therapists that Heidi Rodino could have called in the Chicago area, the coincidence of calling the one whose son had the same condition as her own son is improbable. I can hear my grandmother saying, "Susan, it was meant to be." Heidi needed a vision of light in the vast sea of darkness that was engulfing her. That is serendipity at its most effective level.

Heidi did call for help, and she received much more than she had expected from a very generous mother who shared her similar experience. It *is* a small world, and sometimes we get to encounter the bighearted people in it. It is impossible to predict the sources of support, information, and ideas that will turn up in our lives. Both of these women were open and willing to share information. Had Heidi not mentioned Andrew's situation, she never would have received the information, offer, and support that she so desperately needed.

Postscript

Andrew is now in remission, although the doctors check his other eye often. He recently described the eye that was removed as "broken," in the way that only a child could. Jacob is speaking now and receives special help to continue his communication growth. The family has moved to another suburb, but they will never forget the unbelievable coincidence of their connection to the speech therapist who touched their lives.

Although it's a small world, we just never know who might cross our paths and what they might have to offer us. Therefore, it's a good policy not to prejudge people. Jane Pollak is an artist whose magnificently hand-painted eggs have been featured in magazines, boutiques, and art galleries as well as on the *Today* show. Jane shared her entrepreneurial message in *Soul Proprietor: 101 Lessons from a Lifestyle Entrepreneur* (Publishers Group West, 2001).

EGGS-CELLENT ARTISTRY

"I believe in serendipity," Jane says. "I usually attend my local National Speakers Association chapter meeting, but because it is such a long drive from my home I always stay overnight. This particular time, my preferred hotel had been fully booked, so I ended up at another hotel that had a complementary breakfast.

"The next morning I found a table in the dining area where I could quietly read my book and relax over coffee before the day's event. I really didn't want to talk to anyone, but there was a big breakfast crowd that morning so I wasn't surprised when a woman asked me if she could sit at my table. I made a conscious decision to put down my book and find out why the universe had placed this particular individual in my space. She was older than I, exotically coifed, and bedecked with strands of beads. She might not have been the person I would have chosen to join for breakfast.

" 'What brings you to Massachusetts?' I asked.

'I'm here for my granddaughter's middle school graduation,' she replied. I was hoping for something more interesting. " 'And what brings you here?' she graciously added.

"Ahhhh. At least it wouldn't be all about her. It's

important to note two things here. Only two sentences into the conversation, and already the judgments were flooding my brain. I invalidated this woman's role on earth after one sentence and then readmitted her because she'd shown interest in me. 'I'm here for a meeting of the National Speakers Association. I'm a professional speaker,' I replied.

" 'Oh, what do you speak about?' She was becoming more interesting by the minute.

" 'I'm an artist. I talk about turning your passion into business.'

" 'I'm an artist, too,' she said. The hat of judgment was back on my head.

" 'Really?' Many people think they're artists, so I decided to start with the all-important question that divides the amateurs from the pros. 'Do you sell your work?'

" 'Yes, I do.'

" 'Oh, really? Where?' I asked.

When she said, 'Manhattan, 57th Street,' I got the picture! While my first instinct was to help a 'naïve aspirant to the arts,' the tables were now turned. She was the seasoned artist, and I was in a position to benefit from a New York artist's experience.

" 'What kind of work do you do?' I asked. Although I am not very current on the New York art scene, I hoped to show a modicum of intelligence about her field.

" 'I paint very large canvases with autobiographical materials, then I add stitches to the canvases.'

"Even though my knowledge of contemporary artists is slim, the minute she said, 'stitches,' a bell went off in my head. 'May I ask your name?'

" 'Faith Ringgold.'

" '*Omigod!*' Faith Ringgold is the one contemporary artist whom I really admired and whose work I had seen dozens of times in *The Crafts Report* and *Fiberarts,* two trade magazines for people in the arts. I was ecstatic.

" 'Would you mind waiting here for a minute? I would love to show you what I do.' I ran to the car and grabbed a copy of my first book and my decorated eggs and brought them to our table and placed them before her like an offering at the altar. Faith proceeded to leaf through my book page by page, commenting, smiling, and appreciating my work. I was enthralled."

Jane was self-assured enough to want to show her work, and was not shy about asking Faith if she minded waiting.

"Then I opened up the box of eggs so that she could see the real things. I carry them in a cardboard egg carton, just the way you would pick them up at a supermarket. Although her eyes and her smile delighted me, it was her question that would remain with me. 'How much are they a dozen?'

"No one had ever asked me that question. When I began the craft over 25 years ago, my eggs sold for $8 apiece. With experience, great press, and increased self-esteem, the price had escalated to $250 per egg. The calculator in my head rapidly multiplied that amount times 12. 'Three thousand dollars,' I replied.

"She said, 'If I were you, I would only offer them by the dozen and I would sell them in a glass egg carton.' I never would have thought to package my painted eggs that way. She gave me an idea that was brilliant.

"Had I stayed at the first hotel, had I chosen to read my book, had I not decided to go outside of my comfort zone and initiate a conversation with a total stranger, I would never have met Faith Ringgold and would have missed what turned out to be one of the most exciting and profitable encounters in my career. The world is small. We never know who will cross our paths if we are open to new encounters and are careful not to prejudge others."

Jane experienced a world series of serendipity, and that changed her business. Her decision to be gracious and open brought someone very special into her world—and it's a very small world indeed.

Jane's story brings to mind the Yiddish word for serendipity: *beshert*, literally translated as "meant to be." Jane's decision to put down her book transformed her experience—and her art! When we realize that our attitude, actions, and openness—or the lack thereof—contribute to our success, we can make the conscious decision to be more open and invite opportunity.

Jane's lesson is one that needs to be reiterated: In order to embrace opportunity and become You Never Know It Alls, we need to **lose the prejudgment.** There are many stories in various professions about major sales being lost because of an unfortunate prejudgment. However, the inverse also holds true. Occasionally a great sale is made because one person refused to be a fashion snob and waited on an unlikely looking customer.

SITTIN' ON THE DOCK OF THE BAY CLUB

Jim Gerber, of the Bay Club Marin, grew up in the health club industry. He mentioned a story he had heard that always stuck in his mind as a reminder not to prejudge people.

"We were told of a 'not fancily dressed' man, who could even be described as a shabbily dressed one, who came to visit and tour a health club" Jim explains. "Because he didn't look like a potential customer, the man was ignored. But there was one person on staff who approached him, chatted, and gave the man a full tour. That man ended up buying the club. He fired everyone except the very attentive and nonjudgmental young man.

"I have never forgotten that story and keep it in mind as a guideline. You just can't judge people by their clothes and especially how they look when they work out."

I have heard similar stories from the worlds of real estate, car sales, upscale boutiques, and department stores. A member of the audience at my speech for the Women's Council of Realtors said that it's a mistake to "curb qualify," a term used in real estate. While Jim's is an industry-specific story that is often repeated, such things happen all the time. When I went to a car dealership to look at a Miata, I drove straight from an evening aerobics class and I *definitely* looked it. The salesman never blinked an eye, treating me as if I were wearing designer clothes.

Because it's a small world, the serendipity of the people you meet can result in a wonderful experience like Jane Pollak had. To increase the odds of having such a good experience, it pays to be as nice as you can and be receptive and respectful to everyone.

AN ESCALATING EXPERIENCE

Simma Lieberman, a national speaker and author, had an incredible, truly "small world" encounter in the midst of 20,000 people.

"I just finished giving a program on stress management for a national convention of the American Society for Training and Development," she relates. "Because my workshop was extremely well received, I was feeling so good that I found myself smiling as I got on the escalator. I looked up and my eyes met those of the man on the next step. He asked me where I was from, and when I told him

Berkeley, he said that he had spent some time there and missed it. I added that I was originally from New York—another one of his favorite places. I couldn't see his name badge, so to be polite I asked him where he was from. When he answered 'Argentina,' I said that one of my heroes was from Argentina.

"He seemed surprised. Whether out of curiosity or interest, he wondered who it was. When I told him it was Jacobo Timmerman, the Argentinean activist, he just looked at me. I had no idea if I had crossed a line or said something wrong, but then he broke out in a smile. 'Jacobo Timmerman is my uncle,' he said, as he gave me his card. I couldn't believe it, until I looked at his card and his last name was Timmerman.

"You can't imagine how exciting it was for me to talk to the nephew of someone I admired as a hero for years. His uncle was one of the Desaparecidos, had owned a newspaper, and had survived death squads and imprisonment in Argentina for advocating free speech and press. I was thrilled to learn that he was still alive. His nephew promised that when he returned to Argentina, he would tell his uncle about me.

"When Timmerman got back from the convention, he e-mailed me that his uncle, Jacobo, was quite pleased to learn that his life had impacted the nice woman from Berkeley who was an admirer and to whom he was a hero. I was just elated. That meant so much to me."

Simma now understands just how small the world is. For her message to be relayed to her hero was monumental to her. For the nephew, it was a coincidence that he could not have imagined. There were 20,000 people at that convention . . . and he struck up a conversation with the one person who knew about his uncle and from whom he could bring back a wonderful message.

How did the conversation get started? Simma didn't

initiate it. "After the energy I poured out at my program, I was too tired to even think about talking!" she said.

I asked her if she remembers doing anything that would make it easy for Mr. Timmerman to strike up a conversation.

"You know I was so pleased with my program and the audience response, that I was smiling . . . at myself."

That smile was an invitation that indicated her openness to opportunity and made it possible for this serendipitous meeting to happen.

THE POWDER PUFF ON DEVON

I was in Chicago to give a keynote speech to 1,200 businesspeople pursuing their peak performance. This was my home turf, and the first time that my parents, who were in their eighties, were going to hear me speak.

Two hours before start time we were doing a room and sound check at the Rosemont Auditorium. The concierge, Frank, wanted to be sure we were glitch-free. As we were finishing up, he asked me where I lived. That was an easy question with an easy answer. "San Francisco," I said. "Lovely city," he replied. It could have ended there. I had to change into my speaking clothes and do my makeup, and there was no time for small talk. But I was in my hometown, so I added that I'm a native Chicagoan.

When Frank asked, "What part of the city?" I said I grew up in West Rogers Park.

"No kidding," Frank said. "I used to own a beauty salon there on Devon." He looked vaguely familiar, but I thought it was just the familiar "Chicago look" or maybe a false memory.

By now I was curious. "Which shop?" I asked.

"The Powder Puff," he replied.

My mouth dropped open. "Frank, my mother was your longtime customer, and I went there, too." His words brought back the memories of pink chairs, pink hairnets, pink rollers, and the smell of Aquanet (affectionately known as "Helmet in a Can"). I knew that my mother would be arriving soon and that she would want to see Frank again. In the interim, Frank said that his involvement with beauty and hair care trade shows at the Rosemont turned into his second career.

What a small world! Sure, we were in Chicago, but so were millions of other people. Is it probable that we were connected? No. Possible? Yes.

When my mother arrived, I told her that I had a surprise and took her to his office. When she looked at Frank, her eyes lit up. She kissed him and took his hands in hers. "Frank dear, it's so wonderful to see you," she told him.

"Mrs. R., you look so good. How are you?" he responded.

"I'm getting old, but doing fine," she said. "You know, Frank, my mother loved you. You were always so gentle with her and made her feel beautiful. She always looked forward to seeing you. You made her feel special."

Frank was speechless. He had had no idea of the impact he had on my old and sometimes sickly grandmother. All the conversations, the thank-yous, and the tips from all those years failed to convey what my mother told him that afternoon with a tear in her eye as she journeyed down memory lane with Frank.

We never know what might transpire when we take an extra moment for what seems like mere small talk. Doing this is one of the eight counterintuitive traits of people who have You Never Know! experiences.

Those people who embrace serendipity and experience happy coincidences do not keep an accounting of every second. In *The Secrets of Savvy Networking* I wrote that the best networkers *don't save* nanoseconds. In a lifetime, you may save an hour by doing this. You Never Know It Alls spend the extra moments making small talk and doing little things that can generate big benefits.

Frank was busy that day but he took time to get to know me in spite of the duties on his to-do list. His reward was the convergence of his first and second careers as he realized the contribution he had made to the life of my dear grandmother. If he ever wondered whether his years of setting hair, giving comb-outs, and having conversations with his customers were well spent and successful, Frank learned at the Rosemont Auditorium that the answer was a resounding, *yes!*

It might be a social encounter that helps your business. Or a business event may turn out to be successful because some interaction impacts your life and changes it in a way you could not have predicted or expected. That interaction might not even be in a field that is related to your business.

MINGLING AT THE MANSION

Judy Farley often accompanies her husband, Bill, to The Mansion for the events he organizes for his boss, Hugh Hefner. (Yes, **that** mansion.) Bill had organized a contest for the magazine. (Yes, **that** magazine.) The winner of the contest would get a free trip to Los Angeles and would get to attend a party at the Playboy Mansion. Bill is a vice president of marketing for Playboy Enterprises and president of Playmate Promotion.

As Judy tells it, "Bill always wants to be sure that people are comfortable and usually has so many things to handle that I try to pick up the slack and talk to some of the guests as well. When I realized that the man who had won the contest was standing by himself, I went over to chat with him to make him feel more at ease. I asked him what he did and learned he was contractor who owned his own business. Just by way of small talk, I asked where he was from. When he said 'Palm Beach,' it struck a chord. One of my best friends from my teaching days lived there, and we had not spoken in years.

"Because she came to mind so quickly, I just told him about my friend and that I missed her. To his credit, he asked me her name. Now there are a lot of people who live in Palm Beach County. But I thought it was very nice of him to ask, and, not thinking much of it, I told him her name. He just looked at me . . . blankly. Then he said, 'She is one of my best clients. In fact, her phone number is programmed right here in my cell phone.'

"I can only imagine the look he must have seen on my face. This woman had been a dear friend for years. He just looked at me, handed me his cell phone, and said, 'Why don't you give her a call? Tell her who you're with . . . and where we are!' Then he smiled.

"I never hesitated. I took his phone and placed a call to her after all those years. It was as if we had never stopped talking. She was no longer married to the husband I had met, and things were going well for her. She didn't know my mom had died. We had much to talk about. I took her new number off his cell phone, and we continued the conversation the next day.

"What a small world it is that a contractor from Palm Beach would win a *Playboy* contest and would—through an amazing coincidence—reconnect me with a best friend. My friend and I have since visited each other and resumed our friendship. It made me very glad that I try to help Bill with the PR by talking to the guests at the Playboy Mansion."

Yes, indeed, it is a *small* world—even at the Playboy Mansion. But Judy Farley extended herself on behalf of her husband, in order to make a guest feel comfortable. She offered information by mentioning that she had a friend in his area, knowing that it was just small talk but still a connector. It gave him the opportunity to ask the next question and extend the connection. That is how conversation works, and how the small world of connections is made.

Connections from a first career can successfully impact our lives in ways we never imagined.

FROM MARIN COUNTY, CALIFORNIA, TO KOSOVO

Sherwood Cummins had been the pastor at the Larkspur Redwoods Presbyterian Church for years and kept in touch with many of his former parishioners. Although he is still a minister, he no longer has a parish of his own. He now works as a personal trainer for Recreate, a company that transforms its clients. In many ways, his new "parish" extends beyond an edifice and is truly nondenominational.

"When Jan and I wanted to adopt a child," Sherwood says, "we were told that no birth mother in the United States would see a 62-year-old man as a potential father. So we decided to adopt a child from Romania. We had had our daughter Katarina about 15 months when she said she wanted her baby sister. Ultimately, we were able to adopt her birth sister through the same adoption agency. Katarina went back to Romania with us to get Gabriella.

"We really wanted to find our daughters' birth family to complete the circle of our two families joining together and someday have the girls meet them. We also wanted to do something to make their lives in Romania a little easier, but, with all the red tape, we didn't know how to find them."

Many people in the community knew about the adoptions and had watched the girls acclimate and thrive with their new mom and dad. Jan and Sherwood were very open about the adoptions and encouraged other families who wanted to adopt children.

"Trying to locate and communicate with the our daughters' birth family seemed impossible. At that time, I learned that one of my former parishioners, Kristen Michener, who had been in my youth group at the church, and her fiancé, Michael, were working in Kosovo. They both were here [in Marin county] for a visit, and while they were here, they met our girls.

"Not too long after they returned to work in Kosovo, a young woman from Romania, Dana, came to work at their office. In the course of conversation, Michael just started to talk about the two girls he met in California from Romania. When she asked him what part of Romania they were from, he remembered, and they discovered the Baluta family lived only 10 miles from her family. Yes, it was an amazing small world coincidence! Dana called her father—who was a retired police officer—and asked him to locate their farm. He did. That Easter, Dana went home to Romania, and she and her family went to visit our daughters' birth family and to give them a letter from us and 13 photos of the girls.

"Thanks to the small talk conversation at the office that Michael had with Dana, we discovered how small the world is, and we are now in touch with the Baluta family. A French teacher in their village translates our communications. Some day our daughters will meet their birth family, and our family circle will feel even more complete."

Sherwood Cummins is one of the best communicators I know. He knows many people in our town, and more of us know him. He is one of those people whose ministry is truly open to his network, which is sizeable in both its breadth and its depth. That a former youth group member would stay in touch with him 20 years later is a testimony to a man who gives so much to so many people.

Because he is open about himself, his family, and his life with his clients, former parishioners, and members of the community, a connection was made in Kosovo by a young man about to marry a young woman from Marin County. It's an amazing "small world" coincidence that connected two families across the world. To Sherwood and Jan Cummins, it is the pinnacle of success that evolved from a series of serendipitous events. Their "small world" experience exemplifies a basic tenet of You Never Know! experiences and of life in general: **If you don't put it out there, it can never come back.**

People who have "small world" experiences remain *open* to possibility, share information, make small talk, drop names, and talk to strangers. In each of their stories there is at least one of the eight traits common to You Never Know It Alls. Each story reinforces the idea that "playing one's cards close to the vest," minding one's own business, and not talking to strangers can be counter-productive if we want to embrace the You Never Know! opportunities that are out there waiting for us.

You don't have to be "footloose" to have heard of the game Six Degrees of Kevin Bacon, which plays out the concept of connection through the common links to this prolific actor. The game is predicated on the concept that the people we know in common help create a connection between us.

But, how small a world is it really? Revisiting Stanley Milgram's study on interconnections, Dr. Judith Kleinfeld, a professor of psychology at the University of Alaska, found flaws when she tried to replicate it. According to *Psychology Today,* Dr. Kleinfeld found that "there is a difference between what mathematicians mean by 'small world experiences' and what we mean. The chance of meeting a person who knows someone we know is high for people who travel in similar networks. When an *unlikely* connection occurs, the world does feel small, whether or not the scientific evidence agrees."

The more open we are, the more we talk to people we don't know and the more likely we are to increase our "small world" experiences, which can lead to various forms of success.

RoAne's Reminders

People who are open to opportunity have "small world" experiences, as described in this chapter. In addition, they

- Give information
- Ask questions that might seem silly or odd
- Drop names
- Talk to strangers
- Avoid prejudgments
- Treat people nicely
- Are approachable

Mr. Disney was right. If we want it to be, it's a "small world" after all.

THE KINDNESS OF STRANGERS

History is replete with stories of people whose lives were impacted by kindnesses done for them by people they either didn't know or hardly knew. Those kind people may not have had an agenda or a reason, or even anticipated the results of their actions or words. These are truly the unplanned events that impact us in surprising ways and whose outcomes can motivate us to think beyond ourselves because "you never know" what will come back to you. According to a study at the University of Michigan's Institute for Social Research originally reported in the *Boston Globe*, Dr. Stephanie Brown found evidence to indicate that by helping others, people help themselves, improving their mental health, physical well-being, and even their longevity.[1] Sounds good to me.

Sometimes, help arrives in the form of an event of historic proportions. Sometimes it's not a lifesaving act, but a small or generous gesture made by someone we don't know or don't know very well. In each case, however, the impact on our lives or careers is a change for the better.

A PLACE TO HANG A HAT
AND HANG OUT

Robert Spector, now an acclaimed author, was a New York–based journalist in the 1970s when he decided to leave New York for the much greener pastures of Washington state. He settled in Seattle with hardly any money— "dead broke," as he more aptly puts it. "After months of pounding the pavement, I finally got a paying gig: writing a print ad for the restaurant in the Seattle Hilton. At the meeting to brainstorm the ad, I met the photographer who was going to do the shoot and we hit it off. He invited me to continue the meeting at his nearby suite of offices in Seattle's Pioneer Square."

The photographer, Jerry Gay, had won a Pulitzer Prize and was one of the best photojournalists in the country. To help him, Gay offered Spector an office, an answering service, and use of an IBM Selectric typewriter, which was state-of-the-art in 1978. "I initially refused because I couldn't afford to pay him for any of this," says Robert. "Nevertheless, Jerry was insistent and said he didn't need money anytime soon. Now I had a place from which to write, work, and network—which I did.

"Jerry resurrected my career," recalls Robert. "I began to connect with new clients, meet new colleagues, and begin the Seattle chapter of my writing career. Jerry Gay and I ended up publishing a magazine for a year.

"Jerry's kindness was something that I never forgot. There was no agenda, no 'return the favor' policy . . . just one guy helping another."

Robert Spector and Jerry Gay remain the closest of friends. Robert has since published his best seller, *The Nordstrom Way* (Wiley, 1995), followed by *Amazon.com: Get Big Fast* (HarperBusiness, 2000) and *Anytime, Anywhere* (Perseus, 2002). In 1995, he was invited to lecture to several groups and corporations, and that began his successful new speaking career.

"Recently, Jerry has published a book of his award-winning photos and wanted to explore the lecture circuit as a professional speaker. Because we had stayed in touch over the years, Jerry knew that I was on the lecture circuit, and so he called me for advice."

Robert Spector returned the favor by giving information, leads, and advice on the lecture circuit to Jerry Gay, the kind stranger who had given him a desk and typewriter 25 years earlier. "You never know" how the kindness of strangers might change your life—or save it.

Points to Ponder

What did Robert Spector do or say that prompted the response from a helpful new acquaintance, providing him with a place from which to work? He made the effort to connect with a virtual stranger and was candid about his situation. Rather than showing skepticism, Robert graciously accepted Jerry Gay's offer of the desk, typewriter, and answering service and always remembered his kindness.

Over the years, Robert stayed in touch with Jerry, as their careers and personal lives took them in different directions. Robert was happy to return the favor of the support, information, and leads as Jerry embarked on a professional speaking career.

As for Jerry, he had been kind to a stranger whom he judged to be a good guy. He listened to Robert's story and empathized with his situation. When he realized he could be of assistance, he paid attention to his gut-level assessment that Robert was trustworthy and made a generous offer with no strings attached. Twenty-five years later, his kindness paid off when he received the support he needed from the stranger he had once befriended and helped.

———————————————■———————————————

GOOD SAMARITAN

Mary Haring, who works with me, offered another view as we discussed this chapter. "It's the concept of the Good Samaritan. One of my cousins took her Sunday School lessons to heart. She always said because anybody can be Jesus, we should be kind to everyone, no matter who they are." The surprise hit television show *Joan of Arcadia* is based on a similar premise—that G-d can be anywhere and present him/herself in any form: the cafeteria worker, the guy on the garbage truck, a little girl, or even a fellow student from school. Just the possibility that G-d could be the person next to you promotes different behavior.

Being a Good Samaritan does not necessarily mean making a sacrificial gesture that might be career suicide. A Good Samaritan's acts are often small, thoughtful, generous gestures. When we are kind to strangers (as well as to people we know), it benefits them but it also just feels so good to *do* good. Where your kind acts might lead can't be predicted or guaranteed because You Never Know!

TIME TRAVEL

Patricia Fripp, speech coach and sales trainer, was flying to Oklahoma City to deliver a keynote speech when she struck up a conversation with her seatmate.

"He was a very nice man who told me an extraordinary story of kindness that some could call 'good karma,' " she says. " 'Bob' had been working for a firm he loved. He said he actually looked forward to going to work every day because he enjoyed his job. But the economy impacted his company and he was downsized.

Bob continues the story, "I was devastated and didn't know what to do. I found a woman who was a career repackager and was in the business of helping people find their dream jobs. So I hired her. We learned of a job opening for what sounded like my dream job. But I came in number two, and they hired their first choice. My dream job coach was almost more disappointed than I was. But what can you do?

"After several months, they discovered that the new hire didn't pan out, and they let him go. Because I was number two on the list, they called me and I've been there ever since. After a month or two, it occurred to me that my career coach had not sent me a bill. So I called to remind her. What she said astonished me.

Patricia takes over the story from here, "We never met, but nine years ago, my husband was laid off, and he was almost suicidal. He interviewed with you for a job opening, but you determined it was not the right fit for him. But instead of just letting him leave your office, you had him wait while you called a colleague to recommend that my husband interview with him. He got the job and is still with the company. You never met me, but we never forgot you and your generous act. There is no bill. This one's a thank-you . . . and it's on me."

Patricia commented that what was more interesting was that Bob never thought that making the call to his friend about the packager's husband was a big deal. The demands of modern working life often leave us too busy to take the extra moment to make a call on behalf of someone who could use a little assistance. But Bob *did* take the time. That the career repackager Bob hired would turn out to be the wife of the man he had once helped illustrates the way serendipity works. In this case it worked for two people in similar circumstances because the coincidence was bolstered by the kindness of a stranger, which boomeranged when the original Good Samaritan needed help himself.

Bob's story of serendipity, and the success it yielded, restores my faith in a system that returns and rewards good deeds.

Sometimes the milk of human kindness is good even for those of us who are lactose intolerant.

GOOD MANNERS YIELD GOOD BUSINESS

For Alan Postle, a recreational vehicle and auto broker in Victoria, British Columbia, a kind deed yielded an unexpected and lucrative result.

"My RV and auto broker office is located in a shopping center that includes a supermarket in Victoria, B.C.," Bob explains. "I happened to be near my office entrance when I spotted an elderly woman who had trekked across half of the immense parking lot carrying several bags of groceries. Their weight had obviously tired her out, since she had set them down on the sidewalk and proceeded to wipe the sweat from her brow. I walked over, introduced myself as having an office nearby, giving her my business card as proof of who I was and that my office was in the area, so that she would feel comfortable. I then offered to carry the bags the rest of the way to her car.

"At first she declined, but when I insisted, she let me carry her grocery bags across the parking lot and load them in her car. She then told me that her arms were about to fall off and how grateful she was for my help. She thanked me profusely and then mentioned that she and her husband might be in the market for a van conversion in about three months' time. I never gave it another thought, thinking that she was just trying to be polite. Nevertheless, in three months' time I received a call from the woman—Mrs. Choptiany—and I immediately recognized her distinctive name and voice.

"Sure enough, she and her husband bought a brand-new $78,000 van conversion from me, and I made a sizeable commission. It was very surprising, as I never expected a sale to come from helping a senior citizen with grocery bags. It proved to me that it never hurts to be chivalrous, and sometimes it even pays well!"

Alan Postle never considered that the elderly lady might be a potential customer. He gave her his card just to allay her suspicions about a stranger offering to help her and to confirm his legitimacy. He noticed her struggle and could have simply continued to his office, but he **took the time** to help someone. Alan was just being kind to a stranger, but it turned into a significant sale. Had he not taken the time to be chivalrous, the Choptianys would not have known of him or his business and Alan would not have made such a significant sale.

The flip side of You Never Know! experiences that involve being Good Samaritans ourselves is that we also never know when an unexpected turn of events will require us to seek the assistance of a knowledgeable and **willing** stranger.

THE PORK CHOP CHRONICLES

Growing up, I heard my family's legendary pork chop story many times. We were always told that Dad was a "lucky" guy because of a stranger seated at a nearby table in a restaurant.

My father was a salesman in the paper business in Chicago. In the very old days, many restaurants served the (now politically incorrect) businessman's lunch. On that particular day of infamy, the special was a pork chop with gravy, mashed potatoes, and something that passed for a green vegetable in Chicago of yesteryear, with a slice of apple pie for dessert. How very American for the son of immigrants! Although my father had grown up in a kosher home and ours was, too, we weren't Orthodox Jews. So when Dad's customers ordered the special, so did he.

As the story goes, several forkfuls into the pork chop, my father swallowed a bone and started to choke. He couldn't breathe and began turning blue. A stranger at another table noticed, came up from behind Dad, and performed the Heimlich maneuver on him. The bone was dislodged, and Dad began to breathe again, although he was much weakened by the experience and the fear.

You never know when some stranger will literally rise to the occasion to come to your rescue. That happened more than 50 years ago, and the chances that someone would know the Heimlich maneuver at that time were very small. My mother is now 89 years old and she remembered that the nice man who saved Dad "would not accept a reward, but we did send him a lovely bouquet of flowers." When I asked my mother if she had been present at the lunch, her voice became feisty, sounding younger than she had in years. "Are you crazy? Of course, I wasn't there. If I were there, do you think I would have **let** your father order that damn chop?" You go, Lil!

As for my Dad, he learned his lesson, and never again did he eat a pork chop. And although I eat shellfish, baby back ribs, and an occasional BLT, I never have and never will eat a pork chop!

My father met his Good Samaritan. You never know when the kindness of a stranger might change your life or even save it, and that reflects the success of our humanity.

The act of kindness extended to my father was quite literally lifesaving, but something as ordinary as a conversation can sometimes contributes more than we could ever suppose to someone in need. This, too, can be lifesaving.

A KIND—AND LIFESAVING—WORD

C.N. Pradeep, a chartered engineer who works as a health and safety manager with Bharat Petroleum Corporation in India, had an experience on a business trip that he never could have predicted would take the turn it did. He relates, "I was traveling to Palghat [India] through Coimbatore in the state of Kerala for a business seminar. From Coimbatore, the divisional office arranged for the taxi for me to travel to Palghat. I waited at the airport for quite some time. Then I learned that there was a strike by the private taxi operators and that the journey would have to be undertaken by bus. It was a hot afternoon and I was not looking forward to a bus ride to Palghat. I proceeded to the bus station, cursing my luck all the while, but the sky was a brilliant blue and, for me, it evoked thoughts of eternity and divinity.

"Normally, I talk to my neighbor when I travel and build conversation and friendships easily. But my seatmate seemed lost in his world of deep thoughts. I started reading my book, *Sai Baba,* about one of India's great spiritual leaders who speaks to the unity of all religions, by Howard Murphet. To me, the Western view of life and events has a ring of magic to it that is truly magnetic. This book was especially captivating, as the author's experiences had had great depth, finesse, and understanding.

"After we traveled for a time, my neighbor seemed to come out of his reverie and began a conversation with me.

He must have seen the title of my book because we got to talking about Baba and Christ, two spiritual giants who had provided numerous fascinating experiences to the spiritual teachings of religion. When he told me that he had attempted to meet Baba on several occasions, our topic shifted to the teachings and the divinity of Baba. Our discussions were so absorbing that I never realized that we had reached Palghat!

"When departing I handed him my card and thought that that was the end of the acquaintanceship. All I knew was that he was from Tiruppur and the fact that he was greatly devoted to Baba and often prayed to him.

"I was quite surprised to receive a letter from him some time later. 'Ronald' wrote that he had owned a knitting factory in Tiruppur in the state of Tamil and had done very well for himself, but the slump in the American trade had caused immense losses. He was in a debt trap and had nowhere to go. When we met, he was on his way to Palghat to commit suicide. Our lengthy discussion on Baba totally changed his intention. He had prayed the whole night and returned home the next day feeling fully rejuvenated. He went into the garment export business and is now doing well again.

"In this world, we are not isolated individuals. What we do has an effect on the others. We should never underestimate the power of our actions and interactions. With one small gesture we can change a person's life or even convince him not to end it."

As we travel, many different people cross our paths, and we cross theirs. If there had not been a taxi strike, C.N. Pradeep would not have been on the bus. Had he fallen asleep while reading, he wouldn't have had the conversation with Ronald. Had he taken umbrage at the initial disinterest of his seatmate, Pradeep would not have responded. Had he been preparing for the seminar rather than reading Murphet's book, he may not have given his seatmate a conversation starter. Their conversation, so spiritual in nature, had an impact Pradeep never would have expected. And the result of this kind man taking the time to talk to a stranger was lifesaving. That Ronald returned to his factory, reworked his plans, and revived his interest and instincts to save his business and his life constitute the essence of real success.

But there's another piece of this puzzle. This unhappy stranger held onto Pradeep's business card and was thoughtful enough to write him a note expressing his gratitude. That is the frosting on the kindness cake.

The amount of time some people must spend traveling from one business engagement to another can be an inconvenience. Often they use the time for themselves—to read, work on projects, or watch DVDs. However, occasionally they meet someone who is interesting, open, and helpful.

BANKING ON KINDNESS

A large company can prove to be the inspiration for a good deed when an employee takes the mission statement to heart.

I was meeting with Marilyn Romley, an associate at my local branch of a very big bank, when an elderly woman came over and excused herself. "Sorry, I don't mean to interrupt, but Marilyn dear, I made a little something for you." She handed Marilyn a brown paper bag. Marilyn's eyes lit up and she smiled and thanked Mrs. Connor.

After the woman left, Marilyn said, "Mrs. Connor is in her eighties and although she walks down the hill every day to the shopping center, paying the bills seems to be a bit confusing for her. So I sit with her and Mr. Conner and help them pay their bills. They have one son, but he doesn't live in the area. She is so sweet. She makes me candied almonds, honeyed walnuts, and other treats that I absolutely should not eat . . . but love."

Is this generally considered good use of the bank personnel's time? Not likely—and especially not if you are an efficiency expert responsible for examining time-versus-money issues. But Marilyn takes seriously the bank's customer service message and puts it into action.

Marilyn explained, "My dad is in his eighties and he has me to help him. I just have a soft spot for our older customers and appreciate how some things become more difficult for them as they age."

Several thoughts ran through my mind. I hope that someday, if I should be in need of help with my bills, there will be a person like Marilyn at my bank. I also realized that Marilyn's helping older folks is a service that can only be performed by one person for another. It exemplifies the personal touch at its best. Doing business in a manner that is kindness-efficient rather than time-efficient is risky in today's competitive climate, but the rewards are boundless.

Would Mrs. Connor have received the personalized help she needed if she had been routed through a voice mail system? If she had been steered toward online banking? I doubt it. This is the perfect example of the **human** touch in the midst of our busy, digital world. It made life a little easier for an elderly couple who had been longtime customers of this bank. Their money did not come from dot-com speculation or risky technology investments; theirs is the old kind of money that does not disappear when a bubble goes bust. Guess where they keep a lot of it? Good deeds can morph into good business, and everyone benefits.

Several times I've been asked to speak to private bankers who need to learn the best ways to converse and interact with their wealthy clients. The next time I am requested to deliver a presentation to such a group, instead of offering them a one-hour keynote speech on how to "mingle with the upscale customer," I will simply say, "Ask Marilyn."

Marilyn's kindness generated success that is quantifiable. She increased the bank's customer base of older people, who tend to have accumulated stable and profitable investments, and she's even attracted some customers with newer forms of investment portfolios. This is the kind of customer service that pays off for everyone.

Sometimes the acts of kindness are from strangers. Other times they are kind acts performed by people we know or barely know. They are the You Never Know! experiences that benefit our personal and professional lives.

Some kindnesses are offered purposefully, others appear to be random, and still others are responses to requests for help.

GETTING HIRED WITH A LITTLE HELP FROM STRANGERS

For some people, taking the time to help others is second nature. In his previous careers, Barry Wishner had worked in a nursing home and the food industry. He says, "I received a call from a woman realtor I didn't know, but she knew of me through another contact. Her daughter had graduated from college and was looking for a job in the food industry. But it was in a year of economic belt-tightening, and there didn't appear to be many job openings for her daughter to explore. The woman knew I was connected in the industry and asked if I could make a few calls for her daughter. I did, and she did get a job. They thanked me. That was that.

"Three years later I got another call from the same woman. My initial reaction was that she must have another kid graduating from college who needed some help. I cut to the chase and simply asked what I could do for her.

"Her answer surprised me. 'Nothing,' she said. 'It's what I can do for you and your wife. When we spoke several years ago, you mentioned that your dream was to live in Woodside, California. I never forgot that and what you did for my daughter. I found your dream house. It just came on the market, and we have to act fast!'

"We did and have loved living here for over two decades. She looked out for us for three years. It's funny—I never remembered helping her daughter, but she never forgot."

That's how the world works when we allow the milk of human kindness to flow freely. Barry and Barbara Wishner now live in their dream home, one measure of what could be regarded as success, because of a kind act that was returned. Because we pay attention, listen to the "market," or perceive a problem, we are motivated to find solutions.

When we think about it, we realize that many experiences, events, and aspects in our lives have felt the impact of the kind gestures of others. This might be something as simple as someone holding open a door when we are laden with packages—or as monumental as someone figuratively opening a door to a new career or client. It could be an off-the-cuff comment to someone at an industry event, a compliment paid to another customer in the supermarket, or a thank-you said to a colleague for extra effort on a project, acknowledging the quality of the work. Some kindnesses are not remembered, and others are never forgotten—and sometimes the return on investment is unexpected and fortuitous.

RoAne's Reminders

When we perform a kindness for someone else in our professional life or personal life, we create the possibility that the boon will boomerang—that what we've put out there in the world will return to us. Good things can happen because we

- Are open
- Observe a situation
- Take action
- Lend a hand
- Decide that our agenda is not as important as helping another person
- Pay attention
- Listen to others
- Talk to strangers

IN-KIND DONATIONS

On occasion, nearly everyone does nice things for others, often as the result of automatic responses. To increase the opportunities in our lives and our connections to people and possibilities, we need to increase our awareness of these kindnesses, in both our professional and our personal lives. But there is more we can do.

Kindness Account

Identify the last five kindnesses that were done for you, and how they made you feel. Feel free to expand the list if you need to. If one list is significantly longer than the other, you may want to revisit your actions and deeds.

Kindness Done for You	Your Reaction	Results
1. A former boss referred me to potential client.	Pleasantly surprised	Closed the deal. Sent my ex-boss a gift basket.
2. A neighbor's cousin gave me ideas on how to sell to his industry.		
3.		
4.		
5.		

Kindness You Have Done	Their Reaction	Results
1. Thanked a coworker for his contribution to a project.	He smiled and said he was glad it turned out well	We communicate more often.

2. Let someone
   who only had
   two items go
   ahead of me in
   line at the
   supermarket.

3.

4.

5.

According to Dr. Stephanie Brown's research at the University of Michigan, the things we do that are good for others are also good for our own health, outlook, and well-being. And that is a real measure of success.

NECESSITY IS THE MOTHER (AND FATHER) OF INVENTION

It was a great name for a classic rock group, but I prefer to regard the mothers (and fathers) of invention as those people who respond to needs. Those responses often have results that nobody could have predicted. Some people stumble into their "inventions"; others spend years in undeterred research and experiments.

An odd turn of events can sometimes expand these stories to almost mythic proportions. In some cases, an avocation, interest, or passion becomes a real vocation. Many successful careers, discoveries, and businesses have resulted from a need that was identified, a problem that presented itself for solution, or an opportunity that received the required attention and action. In each case, the person involved invested time, interest, energy, money, and the often-underrated **BST factor** (blood, sweat, and tears—another classic rock group), as well as the other Usual Suspect traits. Each person also exhibited one or more of the *Un*usual Suspects—the eight counterintuitive traits that turned the opportunity they encountered into a success. (See Chapter 1.)

From a surfer's need for a wet suit designed for cold water to the favorite homemade recipe that morphs into a multi-million-dollar business, we just never know where our observations, talents, and interests will lead. Successful discoveries are made everyday by many people in our networks, professions, communities, and families. Asking people how they got to where they are and what happened along the way yields interesting You Never Know! stories.

SURF'S UP

Although he was known worldwide in the surfer community, Jack O'Neill was one of a small group who surfed off Ocean Beach in San Francisco in the late 1950s. Unlike the warm water for surfing in Hawaii, San Francisco's water is often cold. According to *VIA* magazine, to keep warm, O'Neill bought World War II navy frogman suits at the surplus stores. But they fell open at the waist entry and water would get in, displacing the air and creating a hazard. Knowing that he needed a sturdier garment, Jack started to experiment with flexible foam covered by a sheet of glued plastic; however, the material was difficult to work with.[1]

While on a DC-3 passenger plane, he noticed that the material used for the carpet, neoprene, seemed like it would work for his wet suits. And it did. The vests he made flew out of his oceanfront garage store. Although the surfing community was a small one in those days, the word spread among the surfers that there now was a practical wet suit that would keep them warm.

As the popularity of surfing grew, so did the demand for O'Neill's wet suits. His company evolved from a small store in his garage to an international enterprise now run by his adult children, with 70 distributors worldwide. If you drive along the California coast—or any coast around the world—you will see surfers wearing O'Neill gear.

Jack O'Neill had both a hobby and a passion, and he identified a need within this area of interest. He found a way to fulfill that need and has been keeping surfers warm for over 50 years. He still surfs and has also created Stylin' Recyclin', a thrift shop in Santa Cruz, California, which supports Sea Odyssey, a program that introduces grammar school students to the ocean. Jack O'Neill is a true father of invention.

Points to Ponder

Jack O'Neill encountered a problem and discovered a solution. First, he identified his own need and that of other surfers. Then he did research and experimented with materials, determined to design a suit that would make his hobby easier and keep him warm. Finally, he spread the word of his invention through his network of fellow surfers—and generations of surfers everywhere are glad he did.

THE CLIF BAR

Sometimes inventive people are only out to satisfy a basic need like hunger—literally.

In 1990, Gary Erickson set off on a one-day, 175-mile bicycle ride with his buddy Jay. As usual, he packed six energy bars—the only brand on the market at the time. "Halfway though the day, I realized I simply couldn't stomach another unappetizing, sticky, hard-to-digest bar," he said. "Then and there, the epiphany, the inspiration for the Clif ® Bar, was born.

"At the time, I owned a bakery, making homemade calzones and cookies, and I already knew that good food could only come from using high-quality, natural ingredients. So the idea for a new kind of energy bar went from the drawing board to Mom's kitchen, where the first Clif Bar was created using all-natural ingredients. The recipe included an energizing combination of carbohydrates, fiber, and protein made with whole grains, fruit, and beneficial vitamins and minerals. I introduced it to the public in 1992 by what was then known as Kali's Bakery."

The Clif Bar was an instant hit with cyclists and climbers. Distribution began humbly in bike shops, outdoor stores, and natural food markets, but its popularity grew among outdoor adventure seekers of all types. Eventually, Clif Bar distribution expanded nationally to include grocery stores, convenience stores, and other retail outlets.

In 1997, Gary renamed his operation Clif Bar Inc., after his father, Clifford. The company was named one of the nation's fastest-growing private companies by *Inc.* magazine for each of the next four years.

Clif Bar Inc. has created a healthy workplace that has received national attention and honors. Employees have access to a world-class gym and on-site personal training, salon services, car washes, game room, and organic produce delivery. They can also take part in a flexible workweek, volunteer opportunities during the workday, a six-month sabbatical program, financial assistance for first-time homebuyers, and a dependent care assistance program. Dogs and babies are welcome in the office, and casual dress is encouraged daily.

On his web site, Gary tells the story of almost selling his company to a multinational corporation. But he couldn't ignore a stomachache he had that day that turned into an anxiety attack. In order to regain his composure, he started a walk around the block and really thought about his options. When he returned, he realized he didn't want to or have to sell his business. And he didn't!

Gary is a father of invention who determined that he had a need (for a good-tasting energy bar) and the skill to satisfy it. He assessed the potential market of sports enthusiasts who also needed a quick burst of energy and nutrition as they rode, ran, or hiked. His distribution plan was based on direct knowledge of his customers and how to reach them. Gary applied his experience as a baker to create a product he would enjoy eating. He also took the "walk around the block" that gave him the time to think and allowed him to pay attention to the voice in his gut that was making him sick. Rather than follow through with his plan to sell the company, he invested the time to figure out that the voice was telling him not to do it. And Gary Erickson listened and tells his story in *Raising the Bar* (Jossey Bass).

One person's solution proved to be a "dressing" of a different sort.

DRESSING FOR SUCCESS

Renee Unger is currently one of the top 100 entrepreneurs in Canada. Frequently heralded as an award-winning woman-owned business, Renee's Gourmet, selling salad dressings and sauces, had very humble beginnings. Making her homemade salad dressing was an interest as well as a necessity. Renee was a former second-grade teacher and mother of three young girls. "I just loved to cook," she says, "and because I was also allergic to food additives and MSG, I had no choice but to make my own dressings and sauces.

"For the 1984 holiday, I decided that my Christmas and Hanukkah gifts would be jars of my homemade Caesar salad dressing. Several weeks later (when the jars were empty), several people called and asked for more. I told them that I don't sell the dressings and that I only made them for the holidays. When friends asked what I would charge for a jar of dressing, they had my attention. After receiving several more frantic calls from Caesar dressing devotees, I mentioned the dilemma to my husband. Arnie, my then-husband, said that if they want more dressing, I should supply it.

"When I told Arnie that I don't package it, he simply asked me, 'Why not?' Then he said the magic words: that my dressings were better than anything on the market and he was sure they would sell well, and we should go for it." And so the journey toward Renee's Gourmet began.

Renee had some knowledge of running a business because her mother owned The Adorable Hat Shop in Toronto. But running a business that included research, tasting kitchens, distribution channels, focus groups, and supermarket and specialty food industries, as well as government regulations, was brand new to her. And like her dressings, it all had to be created from scratch.

"It was not an easy road to transport an idea from your head to the marketplace," she comments. "Getting the dressings from the kitchen to the public was not an easy task. This involved searching and sourcing raw ingredients that had to end up in a product with a six-month shelf life and be natural and bacteria-free. We had to cost out the dressings; study the marketplace for price, taste, and packaging; and decide on their market position. The competition was the giant Kraft Foods. But 'healthy,' 'fresh,' 'light,' and 'natural' were terms that were just starting to be used and people's consciousness of them was growing."

According to Renee, it's one thing to get the product into supermarkets and quite another to get them into people's refrigerators and, ultimately, their mouths. And she has. From her home kitchen to a 35,000-square-foot facility, Renee's Gourmet is the number one refrigerated dressing in Canada. She is consistently named one of Canada's top female entrepreneurs, and her Extreme Cheese Salad Dressing was named the 2003 Dressing of the Year by the Association of Dressings and Sauces. Renee's Gourmet produces a variety of salad dressings and sauces that are available on supermarket shelves throughout Canada and in the United States. Her daughters and son-in-law as well as her former spouse also work in this family-run enterprise. The necessity of having a salad dressing without the additives turned this mother of three into a mother of invention. Holiday gifts evolved into one heck of a successful business. You just never know!

Renee Unger had the savvy to recognize that her homemade dressing was good enough to give as a holiday gift. When asked what she would charge for it, she heard the *über*message: This is worth good money. She shared her dilemma with her spouse, whose support cannot be overestimated. They were motivated to begin the necessary research and experimentation, investigate the start-up costs, run the financials, and put in the time, money, and sweat equity to build the business. There were obstacles to overcome. She has had to learn finances, build an executive team, develop distribution channels, and be part of the public relations plan for growing the company. Renee Unger, former second-grade teacher, part-time jewelry salesperson, and mother, who loved to cook, had to go outside her comfort zone. She now speaks at conferences, where she shares her story with audiences as well as the media. It wasn't a lucky accident. The Ungers listened to the feedback from their end users and knew they had a great product and the beginnings of a market.

Renee and Arnie Unger worked hard to take her tasty creations to the marketplace. And they still do.

SWIRLING WATERS RUN DEEPER

In this case the beneficiary of an innovation was a single person with a profound problem.

The summer of 1950 was dangerous and debilitating for far too many of us. It was the height of the polio epidemic. Our family left Chicago that summer for what my parents thought was a safer environment. That summer, while we were catching softballs and fireflies, my brother, Michael, caught polio.

It manifested the following November along with spinal meningitis—a potentially deadly combination. Fortunately, in his case the diseases weren't deadly, but they were crippling. After months in the hospital he came home to physical therapy, massage, and the whirlpool water cures similar to those that Franklin Delano Roosevelt, also a polio victim, sought in Warm Springs, Georgia.

Schlepping my brother, who now wore a 30-pound steel brace on his left leg, to physical therapy was a difficult task that had to be done twice a week. The doctor said that daily doses of swirling warm water, much like the hospital whirlpool, would be helpful to the circulation in his leg.

My father knew what he **had** to do. He heard and internalized what the doctor had said about the benefits of the whirlpools. Daily visits to the physical therapists were not possible, so an alternative had to be found. Although he was a salesman by profession, Dad was very good with electronics and was a talented tinkerer. (He turned our hi-fi into a stereo, wired our gutters, and helped me make a Schenley bottle lamp for home economics.) Dad began his research and trials to figure out how he could make our tub into the whirlpool bath my brother needed. My mother commented on that time in their lives, "Nate worked at his day job and also worked late into the night on his tub attachment because he desperately wanted to do something to make life better for our son."

After many trials, he successfully attached a motor to a gizmo and then to the bathtub, creating a makeshift whirling pool to help rehabilitate and strengthen Michael's leg. Because it operated electrically, there was the possibility of an electrical short in the water, so Dad called in an electrical expert to examine it. He wanted to help Michael, not electrocute him! Dr. Aries, Michael's doctor, also came to check it out from a medical perspective.

The word got out and, according to my mother, "A reporter from the *Chicago Sun-Times* came to our apartment to interview and photograph Nate with his invention. The reporter asked him, 'Mr. Rosenberg, how did you even think of it?'

"I'll never forget Nate's answer, 'I had no choice. My son needed some comfort and I didn't know how to give it to him, but I thought this bathtub whirlpool would.' And it did. For over three years, your father bathed Michael nightly because I was afraid I would electrocute him."

Dad accomplished his goal and supervised bath time. He and his invention appeared in the *Chicago Sun-Times* in 1952, giving hope to others who had survived the polio epidemic. My mother still has the article that appeared over 50 years ago. Although he continued to work in his chosen field and later owned Randolph Paper Company, Nate Rosenberg strayed from his career path on his personal time. My dad was a father of invention.

Dad's determination was born out of the strongest motivation—a parent's need to help a suffering child. There would never be an "it can't be done" moment because, for him, that simply wasn't an option. He researched the whirlpools used by physical therapists, sought out the machinery and materials, and worked to duplicate the process and effects on the smaller scale of a bathtub. He worked tirelessly on his project. A born and bred Chicagoan, Dad had a huge support network including family, business associates, clients, and an interesting array of Chicago-based acquaintances who had sources and resources. They were happy to help Nate help the son who had polio. Through his network, Dad located the expert who provided the safety inspection of his invention. As soon as his innovation was declared safe, Michael had his nightly whirlpool baths.

Michael is now a Chicago attorney. He is married, has two grown sons, teaches Sunday school, and is a devoted Cubs and Bulls fan. Today he wears a lighter-weight brace on his left leg. But one thing about him has never changed: his personal devotion over 50 years to the Three Stooges!

A TISKET, A TASKET

People with a given talent or even just a knack for the creative are sometimes able to parlay that into a successful business.

In the past decade, the specialized gift basket industry has flourished. I presented the keynote speech for *Festivities* magazine's jubilee convention in Connecticut, where I met one of the most successful gift basket business owners, Vivian Shiffman. The motivation and means for starting her business constituted a series of serendipitous events.

Vivian explains, "I've always liked being creative and designing baskets of gifts filled with imagination, fun, and goodies for family, friends, and associates for their birthdays, anniversaries, or retirements. But I had a job I liked and no plans to go into the gift basket business. Although my coworkers thought they [my baskets] were really special, and often told me that I was missing my calling, I still had no plans to start a business.

"One day, I was approached by a manager who asked if I was the gal who made the gifts with the large bows. His question made me nervous because we weren't supposed to do that type of thing at work, even on a break. He mentioned that they had someone in their office who was retiring with 38 years service and they had $60 for a gift. Well, $60 in 1974 was a lot of money. Being the shopper that I am, I purchased everything retail and still had approximately $11 left over.

"I managed to get to work really early on the day they requested their gift basket. I stepped onto the elevator, but ended up in the back corner because there were so many people crowding into it. There were 12 floors in the building, and I couldn't get off on my floor because my hands were full and no one was letting me off! But something strange and wonderful started to happen. Everyone who got onto the elevator raved about the basket, saying, 'It must be for me' and other really nice comments. Well, I enjoyed the compliments, but then people asked who made the basket. When I said that I did, they asked for my number. When I finally got off the elevator, I was so thrilled with the feedback that I decided to ride the other five elevators before I made my delivery. The same thing happened.

"When I delivered the gift basket, they were so pleased they let me keep the $11 for my work, and I thought that would be the end of it. But remember, I had given out my work number on the elevators. By 4 P.M., I had 40 orders for the same gift basket. That's when I knew! And my business was born."

Vivian Shiffman is now a successful entrepreneur who is a leader in her industry, has been honored by her peers, and mentors others in the gift basket industry. Vivian took the time to create gifts for family, friends and colleagues, which she did simply because she enjoyed making gift baskets.

She also *listened to* the feedback from the "market" and realized that she needed to supply an answer to the inevitable question "How much would you charge for that?" When the initial ride in the elevator yielded such positive results, she decided that the five other elevators in the bank were prime "marketing" venues. And she rode that horse—er, elevator.

The necessity of giving a gift and the need to express her creativity propelled Vivian Shiffman into her successful business. Creative Gift Basket Services is a full-time, full-service business thanks to a retiring colleague, an astute manager, and elevator small talk.

You never know where finding a solution to a personal need will lead.

FROM BASEMENT TO BOARDROOM

It seems like only yesterday to him, but it was more than 30 years ago when Martin Edelston started Boardroom, Inc., in his basement with $5,000 and a dream.

"At the time," says Martin, "I had many questions about business—how to be more effective at work, how to manage my money—and from experience, I felt that other businessmen were as ignorant. Sound familiar? The issues confronting most Americans now are the same ones that I was grappling with back when my office was at home in the same room as the furnace."

Although access to information has increased with the advent of the Internet, getting specific answers can still be a problem. Martin continues, "I didn't have time to wade through volumes of publications in search of the answers to my questions. The problem, I found back then, was that the information readily available in the popular media didn't answer any of my questions. Or, in the rare instances when an article did provide answers, it did so in such a long-winded, confusing way that I had to read it over and over to somewhat understand what the author was trying to say. I needed the information accurately, concisely, and clearly written. And I needed it fast. And so Boardroom, Inc., and Bottom Line Publications were created out of a need I had and knew others shared. As the competition got keener, I started a newsletter for personal life, as I had as many questions there as I had in business.

"Today, 31 years later, we publish four periodicals and dozens of books dedicated to this quest for the best, most useful, and easy-to-read answers to the many, many challenges of today's fast-paced life. We have a network of thousands of experts who are tops in their fields. We ask them the tough questions and bring you their inside perspectives."

Martin Edelston not only brings you the information and advice of his experts, he also brings his experts together. "There is something that is incredibly creative that occurs when a group of bright people of accomplishment break bread and share ideas," he notes. "To foster those discussions and to be sure we get to meet our experts as well, Boardroom hosts 12 dinners a year, and our experts choose the most convenient one to attend.

While most are from the tri-state area, many come from the Midwest, the South, and the West Coast to brainstorm, converse, and have a great meal and a good time."

Martin Edelston creates networks of people who get to connect, collaborate, and make new friends as well as cheer each other on. Bottom Line serves a huge market, meeting the same needs that Edelston himself had more than three decades ago. He paid attention to his own questions, concerns, and issues, realizing that others shared them, and he sought a way to provide much-needed, concise, expert advice that helps others in their professional and personal lives. With a great idea and lots of brainstorming, effort, energy, and hard work, he created a national success.

Sometimes a business develops not by design, but *because* of it.

DESIGNING WOMAN

Laurel Burch Designs are sold in department stores, boutiques, and gift shops throughout the country. She has expanded her offerings to include multiple products—bags, scarves, linens, mugs, and jewelry—and also has a web site to serve her customers. Sounds impressive—and it is, especially when we consider her beginnings.

When she was young, Laurel would collect beads and stones, fashion them into jewelry, and wear them. As she grew older, if someone noticed and admired a piece of jewelry, she would give it away.

In the 1970s, Laurel Burch was a single mom with two children living in San Francisco. She made colorful and uniquely designed jewelry that she sold on street corners and at street fairs to support herself and her children. People bought her creations and often their friends noticed them and asked where they could buy similar pieces. The word about her designs began to spread. When customers began to ask for her jewelry in department stores and boutiques, the retail market mavens jumped into the picture, contracted to sell pieces, and the rest is fashion history. Naturally, she experienced the usual ups and downs involved in growing a business, but she learned about merchandising, licensing, and production, and her business expanded accordingly, as her creations were sold in department, boutique, and specialty stores.

Because this mother of invention needed to support her young children, Laurel initially made her jewelry at home, during her kids' school hours and after their bedtime. As her business developed, she sought the advice, support, and expertise she needed to grow it into the thriving enterprise it now is. Now, when her schedule permits, she speaks at women's conferences and small business meetings to give back to the community by sharing her story and inspiring others.

Laurel Burch progressed from street seller to big seller. "You never know" where your talent might lead. Today she is an award-winning entrepreneur—a true mother of invention whose business continues to grow.

For other mothers of invention, success is an outgrowth of personal preference.

A SPOT OF TEA HITS THE SPOT

At a recent wedding luncheon in a Silicon Valley restaurant, one of the guests commented on the elegant tea bag and the wonderful aroma of the leaves. "The bag feels like silk," the guest explained to us as she passed it around the table.

I noticed the name and remembered that I had just read about this fairly new company, Mighty Leaf Tea. According to the *San Francisco Chronicle*, husband-and-wife founders, Gary Shinner and Jill Portman had had high-stress corporate jobs in Chicago but always found a moment for "a soothing cup of tea."[2]

Because they determined that tea would be a trend in the 1990s, and that many food trends start in San Francisco, they moved west. First, they owned a teahouse in San Francisco for five years. They wanted to offer a whole-leaf tea that would create a multisensory experience for the customer. To expand that customer base, they founded Mighty Leaf, which now has 5,000 retail accounts in the United States, Canada, and even Asia.

Tea has established a toehold in our U.S. coffee culture. Many luxury hotels now offer high tea for guests seeking a peaceful, elegant, and relaxing respite in the afternoon. Mighty Leaf's owners channeled their relief at their release from the high-stress jobs they formerly held into their passion for a product that offers similar relief to others. From this, they have achieved their goal of creating a successful business.

A request for a product that is not available just might end up launching a nationwide trend.

HAVE A HEART STICKER

Whether we are in a stationery store, a bookstore, a toy store, or even a drugstore, we see racks of them: stickers.

They are used by both children and adults, and are a mainstay of hobbies like scrapbooking.

I love them and use them often. They come in all sizes and shapes and for all occasions. The largest decorative sticker company in America, according to an article in the *Marin Independent Journal,* is now Mrs. Grossman's Stickers, which started as a home stationery business in 1979.[3]

Andrea Grossman was originally a freelance art designer whose stationery was marketed through different local stores. As with so many successful ventures, Mrs. Grossman's Stickers was started as a response to a request. One of the owners of a local stationery store asked Andrea whether she could supply some heart-shaped stickers for Valentine's Day. Although she was not in the sticker business, Andrea said yes. The printing company she used said it could be done, but the minimum order was 50,000. Although that was a huge amount, Andrea Grossman agreed and then had to figure out a plan to sell that many.

The stickers were a hit, but they could only be produced in rolls. Andrea turned that into a positive by creating Mrs. Grossman's slogan: "Stickers by the Yard." The company has expanded its product line to include decorative gift bags, calendars, and activity kits. She continues to design new stickers because there is market demand for them; her customers tell her what kind of stickers they want. Andrea's brilliant marketing strategy is that she *listens* to her market.

What started as a home-based business grew to include a 110,000-square-foot printing factory. Mrs. Grossman's sticking power is unparalleled. Like many businesses, it has endured difficult economic times and emerged stronger. The company is the only sticker company that prints its owns stickers, and the factory tours of Mrs.

Grossman's Stickers are one of the most popular tourist attractions in California's wine country.

The need to fulfill a small customer's request started Andrea Grossman on an odyssey that resulted in cards, notebooks, envelopes, reports, albums, and letters that are sold across the country. Had she not had the vision to see the possibilities of expanding beyond stationery, she might have turned down the request. When she heard the number for a minimum printing order, she could have said "no, thanks." When the business boomed, she might have shied away from the growth opportunities. But she didn't, and now she is in a position to offer growth opportunities to her employees. She has hired developmentally challenged adults as employees and supports a community project whereby young people can learn work skills in the Hunters Point area of San Francisco. Most recently, Andrea has let her business go to the dogs, in a manner of speaking. The canines get to bring their owners to work in an environment that is open, friendly, and productive. You might say that Andrea Grossman is a stickler for success.

Sometimes we need to give parents a way to run with their children instead of running away from them.

HAVE BABY—WILL RUN

I see baby joggers everywhere, so a television interview with Phil Baechler caught my eye one day when I was channel surfing. Phil was saying, "Everyone always asks how I came up with the idea for the Baby Jogger. It was a dark and stormy night and I was working on the copy desk of our local newspaper back in 1983. The only time I could run was during the day. Problem was, that was also the time I had to take care of my infant son, Travis, so my wife, Mary, could work.

"In addition to running, I used to race bicycles and had worked in a bicycle shop, so I put my thinking cap on and envisioned a contraption with big wheels. In my mind, it looked like the opposite of a rickshaw: something to push in front of you while the baby slept."

The interviewer asked Baechler about the venture capital funding for his research and prototyping. He laughed and said that there was none. "I got a vintage 1950s stroller. I thought 20-inch wheels from a kid's bike would be about the right size, so I scrounged up three of those, rust and all, and an old bent Schwinn front from a bike store. It was blue, ugly, heavy, and crude—but it worked! Travis was six months old when I bundled him into it and took him for his first run. The Baby Jogger was born!" People took notice as he ran with Travis and wanted to know how to get one of the contraptions for themselves. Thus, because of a baby being born, a business was, too.

After his father-in-law sent them Phil's promotional brochure, *People* magazine did a one-page story. His father-in-law then showed the magazine article to Armand Hammer, who promptly ordered a Baby Jogger for his friends Prince Charles and Princess Diana. When word got out about that high-profile order, business boomed.

The next time you go to a park or running track, look for Phil's Baby Joggers. Finding a way to continue jogging while caring for his infant son was the problem Phil faced. His solution not only became a royal gift, but made the Baby Jogger a must-have item for moms and dads on the run.

Certain other mothers of invention do not measure success in dollars, but in lives touched, altered, and improved.

SIGNING BONUS

Some independent enterprises are not-for-profit, but are likewise formed out of a necessity that is experienced or observed. And they make a difference.

Thirty years ago, Lois Keenan was a young teacher of hearing-impaired individuals in San Francisco. As she relates it, "I noticed that the parents of my students experienced tremendous difficulty communicating with their children, who were only being taught an oral approach based on lipreading. The frustration was palpable.

"There is a political aspect to this issue in that hearing people in the profession often decided that signing was not good for the hearing-impaired. Joanne, one of my colleagues, who was profoundly deaf, told me that she thought she really was dumb until she learned sign. Joanne's teachers used to slap her hands and those of her deaf classmates when they were caught using sign language. Joanne admitted that her world opened up when she attended Gallaudet University and could sign freely.

"It was there that she learned that although she was deaf, she was smart." Lois Keenan heard and internalized her colleague's comment. In order to communicate with each other, she believed that there was a need for both the parents and the students to learn sign language.

Lois continues, "It seems logical that there was only one way for parents and their hearing-impaired child to learn to communicate well. To me, a sign class was the solution. Because district officials frowned upon sign language, I put my job at risk and secretly taught the class in my home. Yes, it was a job risk, but it was worth it if families could communicate with each other.

"When I moved to the Napa Valley, I was hired as a teacher of the hearing-impaired in Vallejo, California, because they thought I was an 'oralist' [a teacher of lipreading]. Because I knew that total communication—sign language plus lipreading—was inclusive and better served my new students and their families, I again lobbied hard to start one sign class. It was met with resistance, but school district officials reluctantly allowed me to teach one class three decades ago."

Lois Keenan's commitment, vision, and passion serve Solano County, California. The program has grown beyond her expectations. Today there are classes for younger and older children, families, and adults, as well as several classes that include Spanish interpretation. Lois's program for hearing-impaired students has been acclaimed as one of the best in northern California because of the extra benefits she offers.

Inspiration, perseverance, and the desire to serve the needs of the community combined to enable Lois to create this incredible outgrowth of a class initially offered to only a few parents. Taking an unpopular position is a risk. But Lois fought for what she knew would benefit her students and their families. "You never know" where things will lead when we follow our hearts, our smarts, and our passion, focusing on the needs of the end user. Though Lois Keenan's innovation was not a product for sale, she definitely qualifies as a mother of invention!

Let's examine what Lois did to create this valuable program. First, she listened to and internalized what her hearing-impaired colleague said about the frustrations she experienced in the schools. She observed the level of frustration among the parents, who could not communicate with their hearing-impaired children. She bucked authority and was willing to risk her job. She kept her eyes on the prize: meeting the needs of her students, their families, and the community. She invested the time to take classes to improve her signing skills and contributed her time to design, teach, and promote materials for her classes.

Did Lois foresee the way her one sign class would expand into an award-winning countywide program? No. Did she create something with the intent to line her purse with money? Definitely not. She recognized that the commonly held position that hearing-impaired students should not learn sign language was wrong, and she knew she had to do something about it. As a result, Lois Keenan has successfully given thousands of students and parents the gift of total communication for over 30 years.

Mothers and fathers of invention recognize where their missions and passions lie and the necessities that must be served. They know where and why they start their journeys, but they never know—nor often do they dare to dream—where their ventures will lead. Economies change, and some businesses encounter troubles at times, but our mothers and fathers of invention nevertheless find ways to make a difference.

Some of these people had partners or spouses who were part of their support systems, although others did not. Most had some semblance of a network of people that they knew and trusted and who pitched in and helped them turn their vision into reality. We should make sure we have such networks of colleagues, acquaintances, family, and real friends in our lives.

Opportunities surround all of us. Perhaps you are aware of a need to be addressed, a problem to be solved, or a passion to be expressed. If you have ignored it, maybe it's time for a revisit. Take a moment to complete the following exercise. You can make a copy or scan it into your computer. Feel free to expand your lists beyond the five blanks provided.

Knowing a Few of Your Favorite Things Could Be the Beginning of Your Sound of Music!

	What I Do Best	What Skills Does My Job Entail?	What Do I Love Doing?
1.	_____	_____	_____
2.	_____	_____	_____
3.	_____	_____	_____
4.	_____	_____	_____
5.	_____	_____	_____

Take a look at your list and see where there are overlaps. Patterns will emerge. When I taught career management and career change for one particular organization, some of the managers were stumped at the prospect of writing down what they thought they were good at doing. I had them pair up with a colleague so they could tell each other what they did well. This proved to be an illuminating process. We often take for granted what we do well. Hearing someone else's feedback can serve as an indelible reminder. Ask colleagues, friends, and relatives to tell you what they think you do well, and keep a list. Their responses might reinforce your career path or give you the feedback and support to follow another path.

RoAne's Reminders

What makes them unique is that each of these mothers and fathers of invention had a You Never Know! experience that they did *not* ignore. Each exhibited one or more of the eight counterintuitive traits listed in Chapter 1.

They also did *not* have long-standing "vast eternal plans" for the outcomes they accomplished that were punctuated with goals, a fixed focus, and a timeline. In other words, each person stayed open and flexible and

- Responded to an imminent concrete issue or problem
- Allowed themselves to be sidetracked, even distracted, from their chosen paths to explore solutions to these needs and issues
- Internalized the messages they heard, observed, sensed, and researched

---

Necessity sparked these business endeavors created by our mothers and fathers of invention. They employed the Usual Suspects to help them:

- They **observed** situations.
- They **ascertained** that a remedy was needed.
- They **listened** to their intuition.
- They **evaluated** the feedback of others.
- They **took risks.**
- They **reinvented** themselves.
- They **assessed** the opposition.
- They **rallied** the forces.
- They **focused** on the goal.
- They **made a difference** for others.

And most important of all, they persevered!

A Need in Search of a Solution
Is an Opportunity

What issue or problem have you observed, heard, or experienced?

Situation

1. People are commuting/coffee consumption is increasing.

2. _____

3. _____

4. _____

5. _____

Solution

A coffee cart conveniently located near a freeway entrance

_____

_____

_____

_____

STAYING ON AND STRAYING
OFF THE PATH

Revising a lifelong dream takes courage, research, and a willingness to give up something to get something else. Some of us make elaborate—even strategic—plans that we follow, and our best-laid plans turn out to truly *be* the best. Still, there are others who follow two parallel paths with equal fervor and devotion, in spite of the conventional wisdom that following a single path is best. We might pursue a path, but as the journey continues we find our direction changing, and we allow ourselves to follow it. When we are open to serendipity, coincidence, and change, we can experience the successful results in our careers and our personal lives.

Each person who shares a story in this chapter experienced successful results from their You Never Know! situation. As you read their stories, you will be able to identify which of the eight counterintuitive traits each person used to help parlay a possibility into a successful pursuit or, in some cases, pursuits.

Sometimes you just *feel* as if you are weathering a blizzard, but there are other times when you are doing precisely that.

FROM BOOKKEEPER TO BIG BOSS

As the president and CEO of Clearbrook Association, Carl LaMell heads one of the biggest nonprofit organizations in the Chicago area that assists the developmentally challenged. It has a $22 million base and serves 500 children and more than 1,000 families. Carl manages over 500 employees and 1,500 volunteers.

He is an acknowledged leader in the field, heralded by the state of Illinois and honored with his own Day of Recognition by the Rolling Meadows Chamber of Commerce. He was also named Executive of the Year by the State Association. He brings an entrepreneurial spirit to his position and advocates for those who cannot advocate for themselves.

However, this was *not* his preferred profession. Carl elaborates, "After a blizzard-laden winter, I had to make a very tough decision and close the doors of my Chicago restaurant. Believe me, it isn't easy for an entrepreneur to call it quits. And I still had alimony and child support payments to make. I scanned the want ads and found nothing of interest. As you might expect, those impending child support payments loomed large. I had no choice but to reread the ads less critically. I found a small ad for a position as a bookkeeper/accountant for the Victor Neumann Association for the Developmentally Challenged.

"Being a bookkeeper was a very different job than what I had in mind, but I had an accounting background and figured this was temporary. I interviewed and, fortunately, was hired for a job I thought would be a stopgap one.

"The executive director and I hit it off and, after a month, he asked what it would take to keep me there.

Thinking this was just a temporary, stopgap measure and knowing what I wanted and needed to earn, I told him that he couldn't afford me. So he expanded my job beyond the bookkeeping. He involved me in all aspects of the organization and had me consult with the state association. My job description grew as well as my skills. His decision was unique and gutsy because I was the first non–social worker in the field."

At the time, Victor Neumann Association, an inner-city facility, had a base of half a million dollars to serve its clients. Carl brought his longtime Chicago connections and his organization and leadership skills, as well as his business background and entrepreneurial thinking, to his new job and contributed suggestions and ideas in the myriad meetings they conducted. Carl applied himself, working very hard in his new field. He comments, "I had to get involved in the business of the nonprofit, learn about the clients' needs and issues, assist with fundraising and the governmental regulations." Rather than just being the bookkeeper, he became a valued employee and leader in a profession that he just fell into.

When the executive director took a job with the state association, Carl was named to his position. He grew the association, orchestrated the purchase of its first group home facility, and took Victor Neumann to a $10 million base. He became a leading spokesman, successful fundraiser, and lobbyist in the industry. After a decade, he was hired to run Clearbrook Association, where he currently is the president and CEO.

———————————————————■———————————————————

Points to Ponder

After the difficult loss of his restaurant and his dream, Carl wasn't automatically bestowed with a solution to his situation. He had to swallow his pride and find a job that fit—although it was not a fabulous one. He had to re-assess his life, including his goals and responsibilities as a parent, which prompted him to search for a job he thought would be temporary.

When Carl was hired at Victor Neumann, he could have kept his head in the books and stuck to the numbers, but he didn't. He knew nothing about the needs of the devel-opmentally challenged, let alone the government regula-tions, but he forged ahead, studying, asking questions, and learning. He recognized an opportunity, and because he knew his worth, when he was offered the expanded job, he seized it. Two and a half decades later, Carl LaMell continues to make a difference for those who cannot do it for themselves.

STAGES OF A CAREER

Sometimes a person's chosen path splits, and the person boldly decides to take the other branch.

Because his voice, acting talent, and costume design skills had outgrown the needs of the local theater in his hometown in the Midwest, Dan Maddux followed his dream to study acting in New York City. "While studying acting at the American Academy of Dramatic Arts," he relates, "I needed to earn money but did not want to spend my 'wait for the big break' waiting on tables. The school counselor told me that there was an alumnus who had gone to the school in the 1950s who was starting an asso-ciation, and he wanted to hire an acting student. Mrs. New-man decided I was the best person for the job. As assistant to the director, my job was to call payroll people and schmooze in order to increase the membership numbers and attendance at programs. The job description included making cold calls, using listening skills, having a cast-iron stomach to deal with rejection, and knowing how to sell to potential members."

As an actor, Dan had always been very good at knowing his audience and playing to it. This was no different. "Unlike waiting tables," he says, "there were no tips, but there was a steady income and commission: $5 for every person who joined; $25 for each person I convinced to attend a program. Soon I was making so much money my boss cut the commission structure!"

But Dan's efforts paid off. The membership grew, the programs were well attended, and Dan continued his acting classes at night. After two years of auditioning for parts, Dan was offered a job as a costume designer for a theater group. He went to his boss, mentioned the offer, and asked, "What could you do to make my job more interesting so that I would want to stay?"

Dan continues, "When my boss told me that I could travel around the country and work with the association chapters, he had my attention. I always wanted to travel and knew this was a real career opportunity. But I was young and green and had much to learn about conventions—not just planning for them but also how to dress and even how to travel!

"I was a struggling student with no budget for clothes, much less business attire. I had to wear a tie but had no idea how to *tie* one. My roommate had it all figured out: He would pre-tie the ties, and I'd just slip them over my head. There was a problem. My roommate was 6 feet 5 inches, and just guess where the ties hit! Now I'm a more seasoned traveler with over 2.5 million miles under my belt. But on my first plane ride, I not only wasn't seasoned, I was the kid from Kansas who was green—literally!

"Once I was in my seat and buckled up, I listened intently to the safety procedures and was fascinated by the mask and flotation vest. When the plane actually billowed with smoke because the air system overheated, I was terrified, but at least I knew how to use the oxygen mask! After we safely landed, the inflatable vest still fascinated me, so I looked both ways and just put it in my duffel bag. I thought that after surviving my first very frightening flight, I deserved a souvenir.

"I couldn't wait to get to the hotel to try on my inflatable vest. I put it on, stood in front of the mirror, and pulled the cords. The vest blew up and cut off my air supply!

"Once I could breathe again, I was ready to take it off. I felt around for the valve to release the vest and I could find nothing. I panicked. I went to the mirror and began to read the writing on the vest backwards in the mirror. It said that I needed a special valve to release the vest. I didn't have one of those. I read further. It also said that it was a federal offense to remove it from an airplane, which included a fine and prison.

"I sat on the edge of the bed and was so scared that I cried for two hours. It was my first professional job and my first business trip. Now I was probably going to lose my job and maybe even go to prison. I watched the tears roll down these two big pillows, when I noticed a thin strap of nylon between them. I ran around the room until I found the free emery board [which they no longer give you], and I worked on the nylon strap for an hour—until I shaved it down far enough to get the vest off my head!

"I'm embarrassed to admit that I wrapped the vest in a pillowcase and hid it in a nearby stairwell, just in case the authorities came looking for me. I ran back to the room and put on my pants, shoes, my white shirt, and my blazer. I put a leather tie over my head, pulled it up, and tucked the end of it into my pants and I ran over to the Henry B. Gonzalez Convention Center. "Going to my first convention was a trial by fire, but that evening I met so many nice people and had such a good time that I knew this position could possibly turn into more than just a job to support myself. I revised my acting plans and stayed with the American Payroll Association. Another lesson I learned: **Never** again take anything that wasn't mine."

This struggling actor found his niche and is now the executive director of the American Payroll Association. He has increased the membership to 22,000 payroll professionals and has traveled to 48 states and many countries around the world. As he emcees many programs and the Annual Congress, gives presentations, and hosts meetings, Dan is often center stage. The members of his organization are very happy that he managed to hide the flotation vest and not get arrested!

People are sometimes forced off their path by an unfortunate event, but because they remain open to possibility, they are able to find a new one.

FROM CRIMES TO CONES

Customers behave very well at Loard's Ice Cream Parlor in Moraga, California. The place is currently owned by Linda Parsons, a former police officer, and her husband, who is a captain in the Contra Costa County Sheriff's Department. The ice cream parlor has been known for over 50 years for its high-quality handmade ice cream. The booths are original, and the freezers are almost as old.

The problem for Linda Parsons is that she can only scoop with her right hand because her left biceps was irreparably damaged in a drug bust where she took a bullet that resulted in nine surgeries. "The doctors said I was lucky," Linda maintains. "If it had hit a quarter- to a half-inch over, it would have caught my heart and lungs."

According to *San Francisco Chronicle Magazine*, the shoot-out resulted in a 70 percent disability that forced Linda's retirement from a career she really enjoyed.[1]

"When you go through something that traumatic," she says, "you look at the world with different eyes. Some things that seemed important no longer are. Life is precious. Initially, I had a tough time leaving the sheriff's department and giving up my identity as someone who was contributing to the community, and at the same time I was going through post-traumatic stress syndrome. My husband grew up in this community . . . eating Loard's ice cream. We knew that with ice cream, the mom-and-pop operations fare very well. So when the business was up for sale, it felt natural for us to buy it. There's been a 20 percent increase in the sales since we bought it, which is good for an old-fashioned ice cream parlor.

"But I know what is valuable and, in a way, I am contributing to the community every time I scoop our handmade ice cream or make a sundae or a root beer float. I always thought I would stay in my chosen career until retirement age, but the accident changed all that. Now I really enjoy what I am doing."

Linda is very clear about what's really important, and that is the real scoop.

We have all watched enough episodes of *Law and Order, N.Y.P.D. Blue,* and other television cop shows to know that there are risks involved in being a peace officer. Linda Parsons shifted her attitude about her traumatic, life-changing encounter with a bullet and realized she could have lost more than the use of her left biceps. She gave herself permission to move on and into a new phase of her life. She said yes to an opportunity that was very different from the career that she enjoyed but was forced to leave.

We may love what we do, but we never know how long we will get to do it or why. Being open to what was available, interesting, and needed in the community helped Linda move from crime to cones, where seren–*dip*ity has a wonderful, double-scoop, chocolate-covered meaning.

DISASTER TO DALE CARNEGIE TO NEW CAREER

A business failure can force a person to reassess choices, as it did for Will Kintish, of Manchester, England, who returned to pursue a path that he never thought would be his career. But You Never Know!

Will describes how this came about. "I qualified as a CPA in 1971 and joined an accountancy practice, and a few years later I started taking Dale Carnegie classes in public speaking and management as an interesting challenge. In 1988, at the age of 40, I had an opportunity to buy into a client's business, so I mortgaged the family house at 150 percent of the house value! My wife thought I was crazy. The business was going to be my chance to leave accountancy at the age of 52, when the loan would be cleared. I'd be free! I was planning my escape from the work world, but I also continued as a CPA with the accountancy firm.

"All went well in the early years; we made lots of money. But in 1995 it all went wrong, and by late 1997 the business collapsed, leaving me in a huge financial mess. Luckily, I was by then the senior partner in my accountancy practice. But I still wondered what I could do in the interim to replace my business retirement plan that crashed.

"I called my friends at Dale Carnegie and asked if I could study to become a trainer with them. My plan, at that time, was that being a trainer was only going to be a hobby and part-time retirement vocation. They agreed, and for the next two and a half years I spent many hours training and practicing to become a trainer while I continued as an accountant.

"As it happened, in 1999 our firm was taken over by a large national, and in April 2000 I was asked if I'd like to take a redundancy [retirement] package. It took me three minutes to agree. Who knew that when I approached my Dale Carnegie contacts and started to pursue my hobby, two years later my firm would merge and I would be without a position?

"On June 1, 2000, after 35 years practicing accountancy, I set up *kintish*, a training and consultancy company. I had acquired just one client before I started, and three years later I'm proud to boast I've spoken to over 11,000 people; have run in-house workshops for major banks and large, medium, and small accountancy and law firms; and have run a nationwide program. I work 15 hours a day. After my five-year nightmare and all those years not fully happy in my profession, every day feels like my birthday.

"I never would have thought that my business would fail, my firm would be merged, and I would start my own business. To have spent over two years with the best trainers in the United Kingdom learning my new vocation, not knowing I would be using it full-time, surely must be fate or serendipity.

"There's no doubt that had my other venture not collapsed, I probably would now be a partner in a massive company, having to cope with the daily grind, the daily politics, and the daily aggravation from BMW clients! (Bitchers, moaners, and whiners.) But now I own my own business, and I am enjoying my second career far better than the first one."

If Will hadn't tried to expand his skills set and improve his public speaking when he was an accountant with his firm, if he hadn't maintained contact with his Dale

Carnegie connections and devised a plan to work toward a postretirement part-time career/hobby, he would not have been in a position to pursue a new path once his accounting firm merged. Business failure and downsizing are deterrents to any career. The serendipity and great timing of having a potential new career path in process turned a bleak situation into a business success.

Most people stay on their chosen paths in life, but some You Never Know It Alls detour and follow a new path, while others face events and people who deter them from pursuing their chosen paths.

DETOURS AND DETERRENTS

Some people may eventually return to their original path; others may not. For some, the detours occur because of natural circumstances and they turn into successful experiences. Other people are pushed off their paths by various You Never Know! incidents or accidents. Still others stray from their paths as the result of well-intentioned advice or feedback from people who really care about them but somehow manage to lead them astray, so that their guidance actually becomes a deterrent. Occasionally, such people are guided back to where they wanted to be.

Then there are those special people who serve two masters and cannot chose one over the other; with a little serendipity, that can work out successfully, too.

PLETHORA OF PARALLEL PATHS

There are You Never Know It Alls who pursue two paths simultaneously in spite of the generally accepted advice to stay focused and not divide their energy. There are doctors who perform in local orchestras, firefighters who also work as orthopedists and dentists, lawyers and teachers and insurance brokers who perform in community theater, teachers who moonlight as fitness trainers, boutique managers who paint, and novelists who supervise data-processing departments.

Many people acquired teaching credentials because they were told that they would always have something to fall back on. The San Francisco Unified School District's massive layoffs of 1,200 teachers in 1979 disabused me of that notion, because I was one of them. Similarly, some people learned to type while they were waiting for their big break in their chosen field, in order to be self-supporting. Just as often, the people who end up somewhere else, like Dan Maddux, allow themselves to stray from their original paths purposely. To paraphrase Yogi Berra, they came to the fork in the road and took it. But some people prefer to travel parallel paths simultaneously and manage to turn both passions into careers.

Jazz buffs may know of Denny Zeitlin, who is both a noted jazz pianist and a psychiatrist. Alan Smith is also a musician—a trumpet player. When Ella Fitzgerald performed at the Fairmont Hotel's Venetian Room, she always insisted that Alan, whose day job was elementary school principal, back her. A fellow musician commented on how lucky Alan was to have a steady gig as a school principal; one of the school district's superintendents mentioned how lucky Alan was to have a career in which he could (almost literally) "blow off the steam" from the pressure of being a school administrator. Both were right. Yet another multitasking musician was Griggs RoAne, who worked nights in the orchestra pit, playing trombone for well-known Broadway musicals such as *The Wiz*, *Annie Get Your Gun*, and *Annie*, while by day he was a high school band and orchestra teacher.

I know of a juvenile probation officer who deals with some horrific cases and needs to offset this with a more positive environment. So he volunteers with his community's Little League as an administrator and coach. To counteract the burnout and build a business with a completely different focus, he also became an insurance agent so he could help people protect their lives, homes, and belongings. He remarks, "While I often thought of giving up my day job, I never did. Just having the second career balanced the stresses of the juvenile justice system and rejuvenated me."

Some people pursue a path but then stray from it, while others reject the traditional approach of "one career, one path" and embrace two loves, whether the second one is a hobby, an avocation, or another vocation. But sometimes a person is "called" twice.

RADIO DAYS

Father Paul Keenan, of the Archdiocese of New York, has incredible resonance in his voice. It adds timbre to his sermons while celebrating Mass, but it's also perfect for radio. As a child, he always wanted to be on the air. "I used to 'broadcast' from my bedroom, using my lamp as a microphone," he says. "Even when I was officially doing homework, my radio was never off for very long. Growing up in Kansas City, I could listen at night to major stations in places like Detroit, Chicago, Pittsburgh, San Antonio, and New Orleans."

Father Paul vividly remembers the night he tuned in WABC Radio in New York. "WABC was then a Top 40 station—*the* Top 40 station—and I was so excited to pick it up, even through a lot of static. Little did I know that I would one day be in the broadcast lineup of this power-house station. A shy kid like me from out in Missouri? It seemed impossible."

He heard another "calling," that of the priesthood. It was after recovering from a near-fatal illness that Father Paul began to pursue his dream of being a broadcaster. Encouraged by a fellow priest, he enrolled in a broadcasting course. There, he found he really loved talk radio. "In broadcasting school, I realized that, while there's nothing like preaching to a large congregation on weekends, it seemed to me that I could expand the audience for my message by hosting a radio show of my own."

He continues, "Because I was working with the Lower East Side Catholic Area Conference, I was invited to be a guest on the *Religion on the Line* radio show. It was thrilling. After the show, I told the priest/host that if he ever needed a substitute, I was available and that I was looking into getting into radio. He took my card. Out of the blue, six months later, I get a call that the priest had to be away for the summer and recommended me to fill in as cohost. *Religion on the Line,* the highly rated religious news/talk program is on—you guessed it—WABC Radio. From the time the 'On Air' light went on, I was in love with talk radio. What amazed me is how it all fell into place, how it all seemed so natural once I realized that this was the dream of my heart and made myself inwardly available to make that dream come true."

Father Paul remembers literally being "called" to the next phase. He remembers the night he was sitting in his room in his parish rectory when the phone rang. "I picked it up and it was a producer from CBS asking me to do commentary the next morning for the funeral of Jacqueline Kennedy Onassis. I thought it was a practical joke. But when I got to the studio the next morning, there, indeed, were Harry Smith and Paula Zahn; and there I was, coast-to-coast, on CBS Television."

From the pulpit to the radio station to the television studio, serendipity had a place in Father Paul's pursuits. He realized that he had always wanted to be a writer, but just didn't know how. "I had interviewed author June Cotner on the radio," he recalls, "and afterward she asked me if I had ever written anything. I told her that I had written a weekly series of inspirational essays for parish bulletins, and to my amazement, she asked for a sample. Soon, I was sitting in the office of June's literary agent, and before long *Good News for Bad Days*, *Stages of the Soul*, and *Heartstorming* graced the shelves in bookstores." You never know when the right person will ask the right question at the right time and the right opportunity will present itself.

As director of radio ministry of the Archdiocese of New York and in his work as a parish priest at Our Lady of Peace Church in Manhattan, Father Paul's unique combination of ministries has the complete blessing of the church.

"I love it when people describe themselves to me as being shy, and when they tell me there is no way they can fulfill their dream," he comments. "I remember sitting in my classes in college, being afraid to speak up. I'm sure none of my professors ever imagined that the quiet young man sitting in their lectures would go on to interview people like Larry King, Wayne Dyer, Thomas Moore, Dick Cavett, Geraldine Ferraro, Marianne Williamson, and Bill Moyers. Who knew? I know I didn't."

Father Paul Keenan pursues two paths, and they dovetail quite nicely. He was called up to bat—and has been hitting home "radio" runs ever since.

Father Paul's success in both of his "callings" is the result of how he took action when opportunity appeared. He also was open about his interest in radio with a supportive colleague whose advice he followed, and he took the time and invested the energy to study broadcasting while fulfilling his duties as a priest. After his guest appearance on a show, he expressed his pinch-hitting availability to the host. By doing that, he planted a thought, and it turned into the realization of a dream.

Some people continue in their chosen field and yet stray from the traditional path.

TEACHING UNDER THE BIG TOP

"It's true, I really ran away with the circus," reveals Bonnie Katz. "In fact, I not only ran away with Barnum & Bailey, I've also added Cirque du Soleil to my circus resume. But it's not what you think. I don't swallow flaming swords, swing from the trapeze, or ride bareback on elephants."

Bonnie was a New Jersey public school teacher, teaching kindergarten at P.S. 38, the elementary school she had attended. "It was time for me to make a move and, because of friends, I moved to Mill Valley, California. Teaching jobs were scarce, so I pieced together a work routine. I taught jazz dance, tap, and even disco, when a first-grade teaching position opened up at a private school in San Francisco. When the student enrollment dropped, I was laid off and back to square one.

"A friend of mine was running a children's talent agency and needed a receptionist for the summer. Although it was not even close to my chosen profession, the concept of paying my rent made it a very compelling offer. As I answered calls, I learned that California's child labor laws required studio teachers be present as child welfare workers who act as advocates for minors who act, model or perform. I referred callers to the sources they requested until one day a paper passed my desk requesting a studio teacher. I looked at it and thought, 'teacher,' that's what I am. All I needed was state studio accreditation, which I obtained. So I offered myself, and a new phase of my teaching career began. My position is considered to be part of the Alliance of Theatrical and Stage Employees.

"Teaching is my first love. But after a time of teaching with Ringling Brothers, I saw the circus needed a modular school with a head teacher. I discussed it with the ringmaster, wrote the proposal, and became the head teacher and hired other teachers to work with the child performers. While not in the traditional classroom, I've taught foot tumblers from Australia, Mexican trapeze artists, and acrobats from Bulgaria.

"My teaching career has taken me in incredible directions: around the country with the Ringling Brothers circus; to movie sets with Lou Gossett Jr., Robin Williams, and Rae Dawn Chong; and to the San Francisco Ballet as well as musical theater. I'm the teacher and I'm their advocate. When they perform, I'm backstage.

"It's the most exciting career and one I never could have planned. If I hadn't moved from New Jersey, been laid off, said yes to being a receptionist, none of this would have happened. I tell people that I was in the wrong place at the right time . . . and I've had the time of my life."

Bonnie Katz said yes to a part-time position when it was offered, although it was not in her chosen profession, which she loves. She listened to the requests and paid attention to the California child labor law issues. When she saw an opportunity for a stage teacher, she seized it. She did the work to get the appropriate credentials so she could parlay the possibility of being a studio teacher into a full-time career. She works very hard to educate the international students who are part of her very unique classroom—under the big top.

CAREER CHANGERS: PATHFINDERS

As a former teacher, I find career changers who took new paths to be fascinating. It always gives me great comfort to find out about some former teachers who are now well known. In some ways, they are my secret club of role models. Among those who took detours and followed new paths are rock musician Sting, who taught English; Sherry Lansing, head of Paramount Pictures; pundit Bill O'Reilly; Roberta Flack, who's still "killing me softly"; and former secretary of state Madeline Albright—all of whom have done quite well, I might add.

To reiterate, You Never Know It Alls see opportunity and seize it because they are open. They have filtered out those people who could deter them from the paths and possibilities they wish to pursue. If they can do it, so can we.

Some You Never Know It Alls found a path that they stayed on. Others strayed from their original paths and chose the other path when they came to the fork in the road. Some returned to their original dreams, and still others traveled two parallel paths. But they all had people in their lives who supported their dreams and goals.

YEAH! SAYERS—YOU EXTEND A HAND

For more than a decade I have written about the concept of support teams or networks, and the You Never Know It Alls have them. They have in place what Intel Capital's John Hull calls the "preneed network." To increase our "you never know" success, we need the same. Who will remind you to be open to opportunity and give you an assist so that you can step off a current path and recognize the opportunity beckoning from another path? Who will listen to feedback you have received and tell you "that's a great idea—you could really make that work"? Who will say to you what Charles Maloney of Management Concepts told his children: "Never discount the value of serendipity. Life is a series of experiences, and, if you open your life to experience, wonderful opportunities will come along that you never could have planned." Sure wish I had heard that often!

S.A.S.S.

Who are the cheerleaders on your team? They could be mentors, bosses, colleagues, family, friends, siblings, neighbors, school chums, or coworkers. Their comments are not just bromides. They are Yeah! Sayers, and what they do is give us **S.A.S.S.—**"Smart and Selective Support." Bear in mind, they are not just yes-men and -women. They don't merely rubber-stamp ideas we have that seem misguided to them. They don't simply echo our thoughts if they appear to be potentially harmful or foolish to them. They "watch our backs" and protect us— even from ourselves.

The people who give us S.A.S.S. are incredibly important. They are our support teams, the safety nets, which I first mentioned in *The Secrets of Savvy Networking*. They are the people who say—as does my best friend, Lana Teplick, C.P.A.—"Oh, wow!" That's why I call her with good news, as well as seek her advice when I am unsure of how to manage a difficult situation. You Never Know It Alls have support teams that consist of pivotal, pragmatic, and positive people in both their professional and their personal networks.

We can't rely on only one or two people—that's too much of a burden on them. We should line up a starting team that isn't afraid to tell us when our thinking is off-kilter, but we also need our benchwarmers. Excuse me for mixing sports metaphors, but we should also try to have people warming up in the bullpen or on the farm team ready to "go to the show" as advocates or advisors as well as cheerleaders.

A reminder: Because turnabout is fair play, we need to play the same roles for others in our networks of friends, associates, family, clients, and coworkers. It's worth taking a moment to identify those people who are on our team.

Tip: If you are spending a lot of time with someone you don't list in any of these three categories, you may want to reconsider their priority in your schedule.

Naming Names		
The Starting Lineup can always be counted on.	**The Bench-warmers are sometimes there.**	**The Farm Team backs them up, with potential.**

An old song tells us to "accentuate the positive, eliminate the negative, [and] latch on to the superlative. (Oh yes, also skip Mr. In Between.) This is also a basic premise of networking. To be more open to possibilities, stay positive about opportunities, and seize the moments of serendipity, we need to be aware of those people in our professional and personal lives who are *naysayers* and of their *naysayings*.

We can recognize the naysayers by their words. But we also need to listen to the tone of their comments and, when possible, observe their facial feedback and body language. Once we identify their feedback and run it through our filters, we can step back and create the distance we need. That distance will ultimately contribute to our being positively open to possibilities and to capitalizing on coincidences.

The following chart represents just some of the people who can have a negative impact on us and a sample of the comments we might encounter. You may have others to add to the list.

Naysayers/Naysayings

Naysayer	Naysayings
1. Parents	1. "You can't do that!'
2. Spouse	2. "Are you crazy?"
3. Siblings	3. "Do you know how difficult it is?"
4. Offspring	4. "Have you read the statistics?"
5. Coworkers	5. "You'll never support yourself."
6. "Friends"	6. "The competition is fierce."
7. Bosses	7. "You don't have the (talent, skills, credentials, background)."
8. Colleagues	8. "But your degree is in nursing, not sales."
9. Members of your clubs, religious organizations	9. "You're too old to pursue an Olympic medal."
10. "Coaches," counselors, and a cadre of "NO It Alls"	10. "The board of directors will never go for this."

Now that we know who may be raining on our parade and how they create that rain with their negative statements, we need to examine what we do and say to ourselves that can prevent us from "getting soaked." Many of us are hard on ourselves and too aware of what we can't or shouldn't do.

OUR INNER NAYSAYERS

Another way to increase our openness to serendipity is to restrain those nonsupportive voices we hear in our heads. I heard that voice when I went to my first hip-hop dance class and realized that everyone else had the moves and I was the hopeless klutz. All I could think was that I never would get the steps—let alone remember them. But I had to reframe my thoughts. I knew I liked watching VH1 Insomniac Music Theater and found the choreography in the videos to be fluid, energetic, and very cool. So I forced myself to go back to class and get out of my comfort zone. What also motivated me was reading about the findings of a research study that concluded that certain types of dancing were good brain or memory training. (Now if it only would work for finding my keys!) My Inner Naysayer almost stopped me from an experience that has been a challenge. I have dubbed my class the "hip-hop hip replacement class"—it is achingly fun, although I'll never be asked to dance backup in Beyoncé's next video.

I experienced something similar when I was asked to speak to a group of CEOs. My Inner Naysayer (who often sounds like an aunt of mine) reminded me that I had never been a CEO and "what could I possibly say to these Big Kahunas?" Fortunately, Mumsy (Joyce Siegel), one of my Gang of Five, reminded me that I wasn't asked to give a speech on how to run a company but on how to work a room, communicate, interact, and connect—which is my expertise. Yes, she is a Yeah! Sayer.

In *How to Work a Room,* I cited Dr. Pamela Butler's

classic book from the 1980s, *Talking to Yourself* (Sunflower Books, 1983). It was one of the first books on the subject in a field that is now more crowded. Her book is an excellent guide from a noted psychologist for those who want to shut up and shut off their Inner Naysayer. Replace "I can't go to this interview because I am not qualified" with "I have the qualifications and a number of additional skills and experiences for this position." Instead of "I can't go to this event because everyone there already knows each other and is in the same field," say, "I get to meet new people, make connections, and learn more about the industry."

It's not enough to shut up our Inner Naysayer. Seizing serendipity and turning it into success requires both self-support and positive self-talk. Remember, one of the Usual Suspect traits is a great attitude. It's best exemplified by an old story about the young boy who encountered a barn full of manure. While that would be more than slightly off-putting to most, he grabbed a shovel and began digging away with great gusto. When asked why he would do this, the boy replied, "With all this 'manure' [I use this term euphemistically], there has to be a pony in here!"

That is the essence of a positive attitude. It was echoed by several of the You Never Know It Alls who felt that they **deserved** the great job, the interesting twist in their path, or the success of their new business, whether they stayed on their path, strayed from it, or even straddled two paths.

———————————————— ■ ————————————————

RoAne's Reminders

- **Identify *real* needs** (paying rent, child support, or tuition) and factor them into your plans.

- **Cast your net** more widely instead of imposing limits on yourself.
- **Be willing to alter** or amend plans and dreams, and be flexible.
- **Pay attention** to the evolution of your plans and dream, as they can be changed or tweaked into something that works better for you in the long term.
- **Pursue your interests,** even if there has been a "time delay."
- **Identify your Yeah! Sayers and naysayers,** and listen for those phrases that cause rain to fall on your parade.
- **Allocate more time** with the Yeah! Sayers.
- **Understand** that unfortunate circumstances can force us to reroute our paths—often in a better direction.
- **Maintain a positive attitude** about the process and progress of pursuing possible paths.

GET A JOB

You just never know when, where, or how jobs will present themselves. We find them through traditional methods: classified ads, networking, job boards, online postings, and executive search firms or we find our jobs via coincidental circumstances. This chapter, however, focuses on stories of those people who learned of jobs both in uncommon ways and in common ways with uncommon twists. Whether we say it's serendipity or fate or good timing, these stories are lessons for those of us who want to create more You Never Know! unusual opportunities so that a job search successfully culminates in a job or the beginning of a business or even a new career direction. In many ways, each story is an outgrowth of networking that works.

Sometimes we learn of a way to work ourselves into careers through the most surprising venues.

A WAY TO GET A JOB—BAR NONE

Allison Fortini was a dot-commer who was laid off from two consecutive jobs when the companies simply "vanished." This was, unfortunately, common in the period from 2001 to 2002 in the San Francisco Bay Area. Seeing the handwriting on the wall, she decided to work in retail while she assessed her career options. While holding two jobs, Allison pursued a real estate license, at the suggestion of a friend who believed she would be very successful. The night before the exam, she kept her promise and begrudgingly accompanied a single friend to a local watering hole. With the pressure of an early morning exam, Allison decided to leave before it got too late. She says, "As I was walking out, a nice-looking guy started to talk to me. Rather than just walk out, I decided I didn't want to be rude, so I took the time to tell him why I had to leave.

"Joe said he had a friend whose parents were in real estate and that I ought to call him. He gave me the number and I left to go home to study." Allison passed the real estate exam and called Joe's friend, who was cordial and helpful, and explained to her that she ought to get a job as a broker's assistant in order to learn the industry while earning a salary. She says, "I never even considered doing that, as I thought I would just get my license and sell a house. But the next day, I did what he told me and looked through the want ads and saw an opening for a broker's assistant. Based on Joe's friend's advice, I applied and was hired. Never did I suspect that going to the bar that night would become a career move."

My bet is that Joe intended to "put the moves on her"— and he never planned on it being a smart career move for Allison. She appreciated the assistance of both Joe and his friend, and acknowledged their help by thanking them verbally and by sending them each a note.

She has since sold her first house and many more, continues to learn from her mentor, and is now affiliated with his firm. All of this occurred because some guy at a bar tried to meet her and was kind enough to hook her up with a friend who had a connection with real estate. And, most important, Allison was willing to take the time—which was a valuable commodity to her since she needed to study—to make conversation with a stranger in a bar. We can never predict what's in store for us when we leave the house and venture out—even if we do it only grudgingly.

Points to Ponder

What did Allison do that helped her and can help each of us create that You Never Know! moment that can yield successful results?

- She kept her word to a friend.
- She placed herself in a venue full of strangers.
- She responded—politely—to the opening line of someone she didn't know.
- She took the time to explain the reason for her early departure.
- She followed up on the lead and called Joe's friend.
- She *listened*, assessed, and followed the friend's advice.
- She read the newspaper want ads and applied for the job.
- She prepared for the interview.
- She acknowledged the assistance of two strangers who were very generous.
- She apprised them of the results.

All too often people help us and never hear another word about the results. The savvy among us keep those people in the loop as well as acknowledge their assistance. Although it took time, Allison knew it was the right and **proper** thing to send thank-you notes. It inspires further support when people know that their kindnesses are valued. Because Allison shared her reason for leaving the bar and was open about her nervousness about the exam, she allowed Joe to offer assistance. And he stepped up to the plate. If Allison had not kept the promise to a friend, even when it became inconvenient, she would not have been in the bar and might never have learned about the possibility of beginning her career as a broker's assistant.

Sometimes we learn of a way to work ourselves into a job and career in a different venue that is not historical but is, indeed, memorable.

A "GRAM" OF ADVICE

Robert Cohen is a film school graduate of the University of California at Santa Barbara who had been the sound technician on several films. "My wife and I decided to move to Spain since we both speak Spanish. Because we're both beach bums, Barcelona was the obvious destination," he says. Upon leaving, Robert's grandmother told him that Spain was an important place in Jewish culture and history and that he must go to the centuries-old synagogue as a favor to her. How many adult grandchildren "obey" their grandparents? To Robert's credit, he did.

Robert continues, "Moving to a strange and foreign city without a job, apartment, or contact lined up presented a multitude of stresses, which I happily repressed. My

Grandma Milly, however, did not. She actively expressed her concern and warned me of all kinds of potential pitfalls. Grams also told me that if anything happens or if I need help with something, I could go to a synagogue and that the community would help me.

"On the second day after we arrived, my wife, Louisa, and I were passing the Office of Information and decided to ask where the ancient synagogue was located. A kind man printed a map for me and gave us directions to the Jewish quarter. So, on a whim, we went there. Now, I was expecting a dark, ancient, traditionally stark synagogue with some orthodox rabbis and thinkers, protecting the ancient traditions. What we found was entirely more interesting. As we wandered down the crooked and broken alleys we saw no sign of a synagogue, only a small hobbit door with a mezuzah [religious talisman] outside. We ventured in, or should I say 'down,' a narrow staircase into a brilliantly lit, restored ancient room, complete with Roman walls, ancient dye vats, a modern [seventeenth-century] brick vaulted ceiling. Two young Argentineans about our age were there, and they showed us around.

"The floor was covered by raised glass so one could walk freely without disturbing the site. It is known that this building was a twelfth-century synagogue, but it is speculated that it had been a synagogue as far back as the second century, making it the oldest and first synagogue of Europe. My wife, being Argentinean, recognized their distinct accent and asked them where they were from and why they were here. She made an instant connection. It ends up that they were a film director/producer team who had just finished a documentary for the U.N. and were doing research on this ancient synagogue for a future project. They helped found a production company called Multi-Culti and were seeking a sound technician from a different country because they wanted a multicultural team.

"I was ecstatic because that is exactly what I am. Although I am not a particularly religious person, I'm concerned with history. I began to think about the historical events from the biblical beginning, the Inquisition, the diaspora, and the events of my family's life and mine that created this fated chance encounter. The serendipity of two Argentinean documentary filmmakers being in the ancient synagogue on my second day in Barcelona amazed me. Add to that my background in film production, my marriage to a wonderful Argentinean living in California who heard their accent, and the advice of my foreseeing grandmother, and I began to realize what it means to stand on the shoulders of one's ancestors. I also recognize the importance of listening to one's grandmother.

"Gabriel, Daniel, my wife, and I set a date to meet for coffee and discuss potential plans. We met several times, always first at the ancient synagogue, and we quickly became friends. In the meantime, Daniel became a director of the Barcelona Jewish Film Festival and asked me to be the volunteer technical coordinator. We held the closing ceremonies at the famous Gothic cathedral. I coordinated the contracted sound setup, and lo and behold, the manager of the contracted audiovisual company was Argentinean—another convenient coincidence. We arranged an interview with the owner the following Monday, and on Tuesday I was working for him.

"I have been working for them ever since and have traveled all over Spain running sound and lights for some major shows and have plans to travel to Europe on tour with them this spring. I believe that I am the luckiest man in Europe. My Grams doesn't believe in luck; she believes in fate, the *beshert*, and creating your own destiny. I believe in working, and that is exactly what I'm doing—thanks to my Grams and our collective heritage."

It takes **courage to approach strangers**—and incredible

courage to do so in another country, in another language. Robert Cohen realized that if he did not introduce himself to these two men who were doing research he would regret it, and that would be worse than the discomfort of talking to these strangers. Fortunately, his Spanish studies paid off, as he was fluent in the language, able to communicate, and willing to do so. And Louisa recognized a familiar accent and **asked** about it, rather than ignoring something that would create a connection that turned their seren-dipity into success. Because Robert **said yes, and volun-teered** his time to run the sound for the Jewish Film Festival, he was in the right place at the right time to meet his new boss.

Robert got a job in his chosen field because he listened to his Grams, who happens to be my Aunt Milly. Another point to ponder: the joy of a grandmother who felt she imparted some spirit, curiosity, and connection to a grand-son, which, through a series of serendipitous events, turned into a wonderful opportunity for him and a "sound" success.

Postscript

Being involved with this film festival brought Robert back to his film roots, and this year he will also be a judge on the film selection committee.

THE SIGNIFICANCE OF BLUE TYPE

Sometimes a job and career evolve from something that doesn't at first appear to be fabulous, but ends up being right.

What leads to a successful career is maybe something you never imagined could do so. "When I was in graduate school, I used to regularly peruse a nondescript weekly bulletin of part-time job opportunities that circulated in the office of the College of Journalism. It was mimeographed in fuzzy blue type that was still in use circa 1980," said Al Rickard, a Washington, D.C.–based entrepreneur. "One day a short entry caught my eye: 'Part-time position, available to lay out newspapers. Flexible hours; $75–$100 per newspaper.' Since I had plenty of experience laying out my college newspaper at all hours of the night, I thought this was a great way to pick up some extra cash.

"I met with the publisher at his dining room table—he was just starting his business and hadn't yet opened an office. He explained that he was producing 'convention newspapers' for associations. I signed on and laid out many newspapers for the $75 to $100 fees he paid. The pay wasn't very much, but when this publisher later launched an independent newspaper covering the association profession, I was in on the ground floor. I met all the major players in the Washington, D.C., association profession, became editor of the newspaper, and went on to a 20-plus-year career in associations.

"Today I own my own company, Association Vision, which provides P.R., marketing, and publishing services to associations. Paying attention to the job bulletin started the whole process."

Al noticed the small, unglamorous part-time job that used his college skills rather than focusing on *Washington Post* positions. Because he was open to starting out in a different aspect of journalism—doing layouts that led to convention reporting—he now owns a successful business in the association industry.

Al found that college academics were important, but so is keeping a watchful eye for job opportunities that seem unlikely.

Sometimes the finality of college days and the search for a job take precedence over studying for finals. Some people think they are just lucky but . . .

WHAT'S LUCK GOT TO DO WITH IT? (WITH A NOD TO TINA TURNER)

We sat eating sushi at her favorite restaurant, when Nicole Wojtal said that she was "the luckiest girl in the world." That caught my attention and activated my curiosity, so I asked her why.

She replied, "The big joke at our Anthropology Department graduation [from the University of California at Berkeley] is that there just aren't many jobs that require a degree in anthropology. So I knew I had to work just as hard to get a job as I did to get my degree. To increase my qualifications, I stayed for the fifth year and completed my research for a breast cancer project because of my interest in public health issues.

"I often checked the CAL [University of California] job postings, and one day I read a job posting for a research assistant in public health, with research experience. I thought that it was the perfect job for me! The problem was that finals were two weeks away. Rather than go to the parties that weekend, I decided to stay in and draft my resume and cover letter, and I e-mailed it that Monday. So did 80 other people. But they only called 12 of us to do a prescreen phone interview.

"In the phone interview, when I was asked about my career goals, I told the truth, which was scary because I wasn't sure if I would study medicine or public health. There may have been others who really knew what they wanted to be, but I didn't. They called me back to come to UCSF [University of California, San Francisco Medical Center] to interview. This was nerve-racking because I had no idea how to dress. But rather than dress 'Berke-ley student,' I took the time from my studies to buy a styl-ish outfit that was appropriate for an interview. That, too, was a little nerve-racking because I didn't know whether the doctor's project manager would be dressed casually or not. Fortunately, they were also dressed profession-ally, so I fit in.

"The interview went well. I really wanted the job be-cause it would allow me to do project research as well as assist the team. While they interviewed several people and checked references, I still had to study for finals and wait to hear from them."

But that wasn't the end of it for Nicole. She made the time to send a thank-you note.

Once graduation was over, Nicole was invited to sev-eral parties, including one for her friend John. She was close to him and to his mother, who knew about her breast cancer research thesis. John's mom introduced Nicole to John's great aunt, Grace, and mentioned Nicole's research.

"Grace asked me what I was doing and I told her about the job I had interviewed for at UCSF. Then she asked me 'what job?' and told me to send her an e-mail all about it. Her next words really were a surprise—a great surprise.

"When she said, 'I'll call my friends on the board at UCSF,' that was so unexpected. I sent her an e-mail detailing the job, department, etc."

The job world works in mysterious ways. If you guessed that Nicole has the position, you were right. Was it Aunt Grace—or the grace with which Nicole handled the e-mails and interviews? In the Chicago of my upbringing, we learned very early that the people you know play a big role in life.

Nicole Wojtal has a real job, in spite of the anthropology department's long-running "no job" joke. As far as John's great aunt Grace, she received a very long e-mail from

Nicole, who shared all that had happened as well as saying thank you.

Nicole still thinks she's the "luckiest girl," but luck played only a cameo role in this successful job search movie.

Nicole did the *work.* She tracked the job postings, found the "perfect job" and went for it, gave up studying (not an easy decision for a devoted A student), and gave up weekend parties—also not an easy decision. She worked hard on the draft of the resume and cover letter, submitted it in a timely fashion, and followed up. Nicole prepared for the interview, including presenting a grown-up work image by dressing as such.

There are people who would be less open to conversation at a party with a friend's great aunt. Had Nicole not been as warm and open, Aunt Grace may not have invited Nicole to send her an e-mail about the position and never would have offered to call her friends, who just so happened to have been in high places.

Coincidence? Serendipity? Perhaps it was a confluence of circumstances as well as Nicole's "gumption" that resulted in her research assistant's job at the prestigious medical center. And her actions contributed to that career confluence.

Some people get their jobs through a series of serendipitous events and pave the path of possibility by their networking and follow-through.

WINE COUNTRY LIVING

Mary Orlin is an award-winning television producer whose career has been a series of serendipitous successes. Coincidences and kismet pave her path, which has never been a straight line. Many of her experiences are the result of openness, superb networking skills, and the way she interacts with people.

"I can't take no for an answer," she says. "When people told me that it was impossible for me to move into television production from medical sales, it spurred me on. Nine years ago I ended up at CNN producing news and travel segments. When Jon, my husband, who also worked at CNN, was ready to explore new markets and the Internet, he was offered a job in the Silicon Valley. While I really love parts of California, leaving our home, friends, and community was tough. Leaving my job at CNN as a travel producer to start over was daunting. What gave me comfort and a fallback position was my husband's assurance that we would go back to Atlanta if I really wanted to do so.

"There were a few people I knew in the Bay Area from my days at CNN, including some who were publicists and guests on my shows. And there was a chapter of my college alumni club. I knew from my initial career change to television production that I had to put myself out there. Now, with the Internet, it was easier to let people know of my move and that I welcomed their ideas and support.

"***Ask* for help and there's a super chance you'll get it.** I contacted a woman I knew who was aware of my interest in food, a focus for most of my shows. She recommended that I join the San Francisco Professional Food Society (SFPFS), and I did. That was the best advice because it kicked off the series of opportunities I pursued. I went to the meetings and regularly called in to their job listing hotline. One day I heard a listing for a restaurant critic for the *Palo Alto Review.* I had not done formal restaurant reviews, but I had been following some local critics and was not impressed.

"Although it was really fun, the job paid little, meals came out of the budget as my salary, and it was a rigorous interview process. But I pursued it. While it was not monetarily profitable, there were multiple payoffs. It made me quickly learn the area and it refined my reviewing and writing of those reviews. I was able to meet new people and start to get established in the community. And because I went in to work at the office one day a week, I was able to socialize with coworkers.

"At the same time, I also was freelance producing for a local television production company that produced nationally syndicated travel segments to air within local newscasts. One day, I received a broadcast e-mail from an SFPFS member who was writing for a Zagatsurvey and asked for restaurant recommendations on the Peninsula and in the Silicon Valley."

Mary could have ignored the request if she had the WIIFM (What's in it for me?) mentality. Instead she suggested several restaurants that excited her and sent reviews to a woman she didn't know. When Zagatsurvey decided to do a stand-alone section for the Silicon Valley, the woman to whom she had sent the restaurant recommendations e-mailed her about the position. She interviewed on the phone and got the job.

"While I was freelancing at the television production company," Mary continues, "I happened to see the press release for the launch of *Travelocity* magazine. It just so happens that I had interviewed the head of it many times at CNN. I e-mailed him to reintroduce myself. Although I knew the worst thing he could do was say no, it felt like a real risk to put myself out there." Mary, who had several jobs at once, did get the job and was with *Travelocity* magazine until it folded.

"Then a friend of mine from CNN moved back home to the Bay Area," she says. "We stayed in touch and occasionally got together. She had heard of a new wine show being developed and she interviewed for the producer position. When she left the interview, she called me and said it was not right for her, but was perfect for me. She had given them my phone number. They called me the next day. It was only an idea and, at the time, one without funding. I interviewed, stayed in touch, and let the show's developers know I was interested in the producer position and was hired on October 15. I had to hire the staff—all of whom are still with me—and we aired our first show on January 5, 2002.

"At the time, the station where we aired, KNTV, was the independent NBC Bay Area affiliate. I was elated. Through a series of serendipity, networking, and following up on opportunities, I was producing again. And there's one more amazing coincidence/kismet/'meant to be' twist. In December 2001, KNTV was bought by NBC and became NBC11."

That totally changed Mary's market from being just the Silicon Valley to covering eleven Bay Area counties. Her baby, *Wine Country Living*, focuses on the lifestyles of winemakers and their communities. Mary Orlin's show has won a Kudo award for Best Non News Program for television from the American Women in Radio and Television and has been nominated for four regional Emmys. "This all was the farthest thing from my mind when I moved from Atlanta," she comments. "But it happened."

Mary Orlin did more than see opportunities. She truly *seized* them and parlayed twists and turns into an award-winning success. She put herself in the path of opportunity, showed up—both online and in person. Mary worked several freelance jobs at once and pursued a low-paying job for experience and as a means of establishing herself. She maintained contact with her network and she let people know she was open to their ideas and help. Mary followed up on every idea, lead, or contact she received. She offered assistance when asked and said *yes* to something that was low paying when others might have said no. Mary Orlin was alert to opportunity and stayed open to it—in whatever manner it appeared.

Sometimes we are in the "neighborhood" and take the time to drop in on someone—and the timing is perfect.

BAD BACK . . . IN BUSINESS

"When I came back from the Peace Corps in Romania in September 2000 I was having problems with hip arthritis and leg pain," shared Leyla Bentley. "I had found an executive recruitment agency in Roseville and went there to interview and drop off my resume. I did not hear anything from the agency for months even though I called often. I was still looking for a temporary executive assignment as executive director or CEO for a nonprofit.

"When my back was still acting up, my doctor sent me to an acupuncturist in Roseville. I discovered his office was right across the street from the executive recruiting agency. As long as I was in 'the neighborhood,' after my appointment, I popped in to ask if there were any positions available.

"The recruiter that I had signed up with was no longer at the agency and a new recruiter spoke with me. She looked for my resume and could not find it. So I went out to the car, as I always keep a resume in it when I am looking for a job, and brought it in to her. She looked at it and said the words a job hunter loves to hear, 'Gee, just this morning we got a job order for a site director for Center for Elders Independence (CEI), a PACE (Program of All-inclusive Care for the Elderly) in Oakland. Would you be interested in commuting to Oakland?' I agreed if it was three days a week. She arranged a phone interview from

CEI, and they offered me the position on the phone and agreed to let me come three days a week and also pick my days.

"I was the temporary site manager in East Oakland for eight months and trained the permanent site director. I then was offered a position in the organization for the director of communications and fund development and would work in the administration offices in downtown Oakland. I accepted four days a week with one day working at home and have been at CEI ever since.

"That's my story on serendipity. If it were not for my bad back, an acupuncture appointment at an office right across the street from the executive recruiter's office, and that I took the time and stopped in the day a job order had just been received, I would not be working at CEI."

Leyla took the initiative to sign up with an executive recruiter. She prepared for her search by keeping copies of her resume in her car. She also made the in-person visit and connected with a new executive recruiter. Because Leyla was specific about what she wanted, she helped the recruiter place her. The coincidence of her showing up right after the order came in is striking . . . and she struck while the iron was hot.

Sometimes a situation that is out of the norm creates a series of serendipitous opportunities.

THE NIGHT SHIFT . . . IN JOBS

"I had been working as a nurse on the night shift at Mt. Zion Hospital in San Francisco for three years," said Bonnie Edwards. "One night I worked with a nurse that I knew in passing, but we had never worked together before because we usually worked on different floors. It happened to be her last night, as she was leaving to start a new job at UCSF's hospital. We had a good night on the floor and no patient emergencies, so we actually had a little time to talk. That rarely happens, as we always were too busy with patients to talk on that shift. She told me all about her new job, which would be in the field of genetics, prenatal diagnosis, and ultrasound. At the end of the shift, I wished her luck. But I happened to be so intrigued by her new job that I asked her to keep me in mind if they ever needed more help, as I felt that I was ready for something new. I never expected a call but I had to mention my interest . . . just in case.

"Out of the blue, two months later she called me. I had completely forgotten about our conversation. She told me that the job wasn't working out for her—for a variety of reasons. She then asked if I'd be interested in replacing her. Interested? I was thrilled! It just all seemed so 'meant to be.' When I had mentioned my interest to her, I had thought she might hear of a similar job. It never crossed my mind that the perfect job she described would be mine. There were so many factors of serendipity that seemed to fall into place."

Bonnie had never worked with the other nurse until her very last night on the job. Having time to talk rarely occurred on that shift. If she had not casually expressed an interest in future openings, the nurse probably would never have thought to call Bonnie. That new job led to a whole new and exciting development in her nursing career and 17 years later, Bonnie Edwards is still there.

A coincidental conversation, expressing interest in someone's new venture, can create a shift in serendipity that turns into a career success.

Sometimes circumstances are so coincidental that they are almost Rod Serling eerie.

PART-TIME JOB = PERFECT SOLUTION

Shelly Berger is the office manager for a periodontist in the Chicago suburbs. "My boss asked me if I wanted to work additional hours," she relates. "He only wanted me to cover the phone in the office on Monday and Thursday mornings from 9 to 12 because we were getting complaints from patients that they were getting an answering machine due to our short hours. The deal was he would only pay me minimum wage rather than my normal hourly wage, so I really wasn't interested and declined the additional hours.

"That very night I was meeting my friend Bobbie for dinner and she was bringing her friend Sharon, whom I had never met. After being introduced, Sharon asked me if I was coming from work. When I told her that I was, she said, 'I would love to find a job, too, but I only want to work on *Monday and Thursday mornings from 9 to 12*.'"

"I was blown away and told her, 'Boy, have I got a job for you!' I quickly called my boss and told him to call her right away. Sharon has done a terrific job for us and is ready and willing to fill in for me whenever I go away or just have to take a day off. She wants no other job and that makes it nice, as she has no other work obligations."

The serendipity of Shelly meeting Bobbie's friend, who would want to work the exact hours on the two mornings that the office needed coverage, is an amazing coincidence.

Sharon has the job and hours she wanted because she was open about her desire for a part-time job. She was willing to make small talk with her friend's friend and ask a question to start the conversation. Sharon was open to revealing her very unique, specific availability that seemed a bit odd and may not have worked for any potential employer. And Shelly Berger paid attention to her boss's office needs and, while it didn't work for her, she made the perfect match for everyone concerned.

Sometimes a situation has an impact, and we make a decision based on our gut that can alter our career.

THE HOLIDAY INNS-BRUCK

Ever wonder how people in the news business came to be on the air? Each person has his or her own story, of course. For award-winning radio news veteran Betsy Rosenberg, it was a series of serendipitous events that led to her unlikely career success.

"I was a psychology major transferring from San Diego State," she remembers, "hoping to get accepted to University of California at Berkeley, when fate intervened. My mother had died tragically in 1974 and, before she passed away, she told me she was leaving my siblings and me each a small sum of money to use for a trip or an adventure. So I did.

"My boyfriend and I took off for Europe on what was supposed to be a two- to three-month trip. With my mother's money and a copy of *Europe on Ten Dollars a Day*, we bought a used Volkswagen van and toured through several countries before making a fateful stop in Munich to pick up our mail. Among the items was the acceptance letter from U.C. Berkeley, confirming that I could begin classes in a mere six weeks.

"But instead of returning home, we decided to head to Innsbruck, in neighboring Austria, because we'd heard they were hiring Americans to work for ABC Sports during the upcoming Winter Olympic Games. In Innsbruck, we learned that ABC brass were staying at the Holiday Inn, so we started hanging around the lobby, which was a lot warmer than our van in the December Alps snow."

"One evening I was sitting in the lobby fireplace when sportscaster Jim Lampley strolled by in boxer shorts, carrying a towel. [He] appeared to be heading for the front door and snowy darkness outside. I made some smart-aleck comment about his attire, and he stopped to chat. Turned out he was looking for the sauna and had taken a wrong turn. He asked if I worked for ABC and when I replied, "Not yet,". he invited my boyfriend and me upstairs to the bar to meet his bosses. They turned out to be Roone Arledge, Chuck Howard, Don Ohlmeyer, and Geoff Mason, indeed the top brass at ABC Sports at that time."

"After chatting at the bar for a few minutes, they offered us jobs on the spot—truly a case of right time, right place. Although I had a gofer job, mostly logging tapes in the studio, my boyfriend was appointed 'transportation direc-tor' for the ABC crew at the Holiday Inn. It was his job to call a taxi, limo, or helicopter to ferry the execs out to game venues. Perhaps more importantly, he was trusted with coveted event tickets to hold for wives, friends, and others who often didn't show up, giving us front-row seats to see Dorothy Hamill go for the gold in figure skat-ing. Pretty heady stuff for a 19-year-old self-admitted 'sports buff-oon!'

"I ended up deferring my entrance to Berkeley, and we stayed in Europe to follow ABC around doing gofer work, and wound up working in Montreal for the Summer Olympics. Working for the crew at ABC Sports and hang-ing out with the likes of Howard Cosell was great fun, and they even offered me a job back in New York. Only one problem—actually two: I was not, and am still not, a sports fan, and I felt I needed to get back to college. But I was bitten by the broadcasting bug, and there was no going back to studying in university psych classes.

"Once at Berkeley, I realized that, however great the connections at ABC, I could not envision a career in sports broadcasting. But I loved news and decided to change my major to journalism and get into the graduate broadcast journalism program, and that has been my career.

"Sometimes tragic events do have a silver lining. In hindsight, I realize that my mother's advice was her going away present to me. Had she not told me to have an adventure, I never would have gone to Europe, met up with ABC Sports, or ended up on the air in a business that didn't have a lot of women broadcasters at that time. To this day, when people compliment my voice and inflected delivery, I smile and look upward, knowing that this natural gift never would have found itself onto the radio if it hadn't been for several serendipitous, and, I would say, magical, turns."

Who could have foreseen all of this unfolding—just because she was in the right place at the right time and said the right thing to a guy in boxers on a snowy night far from home? Not Betsy! All she knows is she *never* could have planned this path. But stay tuned . . . she's not finished yet.

Although Betsy thinks it's magical, a closer look reveals the actions that she took to create her You Never Know! success. First of all, she took her mother's dying wish to heart. In Europe, Betsy and her beau had met and stayed in touch with other young Americans who were traveling in Europe, and when they heard—through that grapevine—that ABC was hiring, they didn't return to the United States. They chose to drive to Innsbruck and knowingly place themselves in the path of opportunity by going to the lobby of the ABC-TV Holiday Inn headquarters. When she saw the man dressed "strangely" for a snowy, cold night, Betsy took the risk of speaking to the stranger and her "sassy" remark opened a conversation that led to an invite that they accepted.

It's important to note that Betsy and her beau worked hard, were reliable, and did a good job—or they wouldn't have been asked to work the Montreal games. She made some tough decisions and walked away from a job offer in order to return to school, change her major, and pursue her degree to develop her journalistic skills—and she ultimately found a career. "Who would have thought a chance encounter and invitation in the lobby of a Holiday Inn halfway around the world would have changed my college, career path, and life?" she asks.

Finding a job is a job in and of itself. It's never easy and creates an incredible amount of internal and external pressure. It's worth thinking about the ways we found out about our past jobs. I'm sure that some of them happened because of other people—and in interesting ways. But sometimes the way we get a job is so out of the ordinary that we call it "luck"—for lack of a better word. When we take a second look, however, we find that serendipity played an initial role . . . and hard work, action, and follow-up played even greater roles for You Never Know It Alls. While they demonstrated the Usual Suspect traits, they also—to a one—exhibited one or more of the eight counterintuitive traits.

THE JOB HUNT

The recurring theme throughout this chapter and this book is that the You Never Know It Alls are open—to people, circumstances, events, job postings, and even the want ads. Because of their openness, they have more opportunities. Many of these opportunities present themselves at events, as a by-product of small talk and casual conversation. The personal touch and face-to-face communication play important roles in job search serendipity. According to the *San Francisco Chronicle,* Dr. Monisha Pusapathi is a psychology professor at the University of Utah whose research on cell phone conversations yielded this conclusion: "The way we talk, we're optimized for face to face conversations, and there are a whole bunch of signals that help us do that at every level."[1]

How to Work a Room was written as a response to an attendee in a career change class I conducted more than two decades ago. Rather than tell the class to do informational interviewing to learn about other careers, I advised them to research new fields by going to professional events in their areas of interest and meet, mingle, and converse with members. That way they would have access to a roomful of sources and contacts, get information about the field, and not waste a person's workplace time. Plus, people are more open when they have a beverage in one hand. One very loquacious student swore she couldn't talk to strangers. As she had talked for the entire three nights of the course, I found her comments peculiar. But once I remembered the finding of psychologist Dr. Philip Zimbardo that 93 percent of American adults self-identify as shy, her comments made sense. It inspired me to address the issue in that class, in my keynotes speeches, and in my books. Here is a synopsis for those who want to increase You Never Know! career opportunities.

A How-to Guide for Job Search and Seizure

1. **Identify your networks.** Write down the categories (classmates, coworkers—present and former, bosses, customers, colleagues, friends, family, relatives of relatives, fellow hobbyists, and members of professional, charity, or religious groups) and the names of the people in those groups. Notice where there are overlaps and where there are gaps. Remember, your contacts have networks and their networks have networks of colleagues, associates, clients, coworkers, neighbors, friends, relatives, and so on. While the social research indicates that there are only 5.5 degrees of separation between people, in many cases it can be less. **Tell *everyone* (including the butcher, the baker, and the candlestick maker) you know about your job search.**

2. **It's important that the gaps are filled.** Seek out the people you need and want to meet and place yourself in situations where that is likely to happen (the art gallery, the climbing wall, the job fair, the golf course, the trade show, the American Cancer Society fund-raiser, the shareholders meeting).

3. **Check job postings,** online job boards, and the newspaper's want ads.

4. **Use the American Society of Association Executives web site** to identify the local chapters of the more than 55,000 associations of people in varying industries and interest groups.

5. **Sign up for a local meeting** of any groups that seem of interest.

6. **"Work" the room:**
   - Have a **7- to 9-second self-introduction** prepared so you don't have to rely on others to introduce you.
   - Read your local and a national newspaper and have **3 to 5 conversation topics prepared** in case you run out of something to talk about.
   - Listen. People tell you what they want to talk about.
   - Bring business cards and be sure they can be easily read.
   - Prepare questions about the industry, ask about the training required and the skills and experiences that are needed.
   - Bring a small spiral-bound notebook in case you need to take notes.
   - Let people know about your interest in opportunities that might be on their radar screens, as Sharon did with Shelly, and as Bonnie also did.
   - Follow up with any idea or leads that make sense to you, as Betsy did.
   - Plan face-to-face follow-up with sources and contacts, as Leyla did.
   - Keep your sources in the loop, as Mary did.
   - ***Dare* to be different:** If every other job seeker is sending an e-mail because it's an easier and faster way to express appreciation, buy a good pen and some Crane stationery and **send a *handwritten* note.** You will be far more memorable.

Join professional associations and **be active.** Being known among colleagues, vendors, and competitors as reliable and competent is insurance. People are not as open to the person who shows up only when in need of career support.

One way to learn about a career and increase the coincidences and job opportunities is to **volunteer for a non-profit,** doing what you might like to pursue while building your resume, as Robert did at the film festival. Working with other volunteers with whom you have something in common expands your network and circle of opportunity. One in-demand professional organizer of my acquaintance started her "career" as a volunteer with the Junior League, working on their charity events. Her organizational skills were finely honed and respected as a fund-raising volunteer, so she was able to morph them into the basis for her business.

On the wildly popular television comedy *Friends*, when Chandler wanted to explore a career in advertising he became an "older" intern so he could get experience in that field and add it to his resume. The lesson we learn from our "Friend" is that sometimes we have to swallow our pride in order to give something new a try.

Sometimes we get jobs that we pursued, and sometimes we bump into them by accident.

RoAne's Reminders

It's a popular myth that 80 percent of the jobs are in the "hidden" job market . . . and we can only find them through networking . . . and we shouldn't focus energy or time on the 20 percent of jobs that are listed in want ads or postings. *Not true.*

- **Don't ignore those jobs** that are in search of a job seeker. Often, they are written like a wish list—but you may still qualify if you have transferable skills from other experiences. So read the postings like Nicole did, and skim the want ads like Alison and Al did. They will give you a sense of what's available, what the job entails, the experience required, and what it pays.
- **Become a Star Researcher.** If you see someone who has an interesting job, ask how they learned about it, prepared for it, qualified for it. Like Bonnie did, let them know you are interested in hearing about opportunities.
- **Be visible,** be present, be polite, be fun, be interesting, be interested, and be **open.**
- To be a You Never Know It All and get the job, **practice the eight traits:**
  Talk to strangers.
  Make (very) small talk.
  Drop names.
  Listen and eavesdrop.
  Ask for and offer help.
  Stray from your path.
  Exit graciously.
  Say yes . . . even if you really want to say no.

HAPPY ACCIDENTS

While some things happen coincidentally and others incidentally, there are those events in life that happen accidentally. They aren't planned and, in some cases, are surprising and maybe even painful events. You Never Know It Alls often have "happy" accidents, both figuratively and literally, which stem from events that involve cars, jobs, introductions, meetings, or even bodily harm.

My idea of fortuitous "bodily harm" comes from the happiest accident in history. That was the auspicious day that someone "accidentally" dropped peanut butter into a vat of chocolate. As the story goes, one of the chocolatiers was horrified and wanted to dispose of the ruined vat. As the peanut butter was being retrieved, some **brilliant** person became curious and decided to taste it. It was the "elixir of the gods" . . . and he demanded that the chocolate not be thrown out. The perfect marriage had been consummated—in the world of candy: chocolate-covered peanut butter. To me, that is a huge success extracted from a very happy accident. I imagine other fans of Reese's Peanut Butter Cups would heartily agree.

Oh! The "bodily harm" part comes from eating far too

many of these delicacies as rewards for writing a paragraph or a page.

Seriously, so many of the miraculous inventions and scientific and medical discoveries have come about as a by-product—as a secondary platform, not as the original purpose. From Silly Putty to rubber for tires, the accidental discoveries were then moved to the front burner.

THE SECOND-HAPPIEST ACCIDENT

A drug was being tested to treat angina pectoris (chest pain due to coronary artery disease) because the mechanism through which it works dilates the blood vessels. However, the drug wasn't working that well as a treatment for the condition and the researchers were ready to abandon the project when someone noticed that many of the men in the studies were "complaining" about a "very noticeable" side effect. According to Dr. Richard Siegel, of Pfizer, Inc., "When the researchers started to examine this 'complaint' [erections], it turned out that there was a good physiologic reason that this was happening, and the project took off in a completely different direction." The end result was a medicine that was never advertised for coronary disease relief: Viagra.

You Never Know! stories tell tales of serendipity, and the way I learned about Dr. Siegel, from my friend and fellow author Robert Spector, was no different. I mentioned that I was including the Viagra story in this book and that I had either heard or read it and never forgot (unlike the problem of remembering where I put my keys last night). You can imagine my surprise when Robert said, "I know that story. One of my dear friends from Franklin & Marshall College, Dr. Richard Siegel, heads the Viagra Clinical Team at Pfizer. We met in 1965 as college freshmen living in the same dormitory and have been friends ever

since. He told that story at our 30-year college reunion."
Robert e-mailed Dr. Siegel to verify the story, and the doctor was kind enough to respond.

Happy accidents that yield some semblance of success
come in many forms. Mentioning this chapter and the
Viagra story to Robert yielded a source from him that I
never would have expected. The lesson is clear. **The more
information we give out, the better our chances for a
positive return.** We get back more information than we
possibly could have imagined. Playing our cards close to
the vest may seem appropriate in poker, but it can limit
our opportunities.

SCIENCE FAIR PLAY

The scientific community is now more aware of how
important it is to share research, platforms, and secondary usages. Because of these possibilities, research
institutions at CalTech, Stanford, MIT, UCSF, and the
University of Michigan now have a new watchword—
interdisciplinary collaboration—according to the *San
Francisco Chronicle*'s science editor, David Perlman.[1] This
is no surprise to me, as Monsanto hired me over a decade
ago to teach communication and networking to a group of
the scientists so they could learn how to better share
information. My client, Dr. David Sikora, was keenly
aware that experiments were being duplicated and that
meant money wasted—because people were *not* dis-
cussing their ideas, suppositions, and research findings.

We can learn from scientists, who need to communicate
what they are doing, the results of their work and the
possible implications for applications in other branches
of science and medicine. For example, Revimid, a cousin
to thalidomide, a morning-sickness drug that caused
birth defects in pregnant women, is in the news. It's now

marketed as Thalomid, which was approved to treat lep-
rosy but is being used for treatment of cancer of the bone
marrow. Doctors realized that thalidomide caused birth
defects because it blocked the growth of new blood vessels in a developing embryo. Coincidentally, it was this
exact property that struck the current researchers as one
that would stop the flow of blood to life-threatening
tumors, according to Daniel Rosenberg of the *Wall Street
Journal*.[2] At this time, there are several trials under way
by Celgene, maker of Revimid, that could have a significant impact on the battle with cancer. And that would be
a most happy, lifesaving, curative result of a research
"accident." As with science and medical discoveries, when
we can increase our levels of communication and collaboration, we increase the You Never Know! opportunities
that can improve the quality of life.

Repurposing discoveries, drugs, and inventions is a way
of seizing serendipity and maximizing it for the benefit of
the population. CNET News.com recently reported that
Ian C. MacMillan, the director of the Sol C. Snider Entrepreneurial Center at Wharton, said, "Crossover applications depend largely on serendipity. You have to hang
around 15 years for someone to see the connections."[3]

According to the article from CNET News, to overcome
those problems, MacMillan, along with Steven Kim-
brough, Wharton professor of operations and information
management, and John Ranieri, a vice president at
DuPont, have developed a patented process that will help
companies analyze databases of information about new
technologies and will suggest new markets. They call that
process a "serendipity generator." Kevlar is a classic
example of this. It was originally used for tires because it
is bulletproof and fire resistant. Some four decades later,
it's used to make tornado-resistant home shelters. Discovering a "serendipity generator" decreases the time it
takes to find new markets and uses for products.

When we are open and pay attention to signs, signals, situations, and people, we are building our own internal serendipity generators.

The scientific community leveraged an existing drug for a new use as what is now called Thalomid. This formula has application to our lives and careers because many of our skills are transferable in the way pharmaceuticals can be. A criminal defense attorney can also utilize her persuasive speaking skills—used in addressing juries—by teaching those skills to colleagues through a bar association program. Or she can take those skills and coach executives who have to make presentations to their boards of directors. Or she can consult with prosecuting attorneys at the municipal, state, or federal level to prepare them to counter jury reactions to persuasive closing arguments.

The computer animator who works on movies can apply his skills to educational software products that also require graphic design and animation skills. The accountant can repurpose his mathematical prowess by teaching math, accounting, or finances at the high school or community college level. The teacher of English can transfer those skills to the field of technical writing and editing. The stay-at-home parent who volunteers and plans fund-raisers for local community organizations can repackage her skills for a career in event planning (for pay). The sales professional can redirect his skills in the position of a director of development for a university, not-for-profit organization, or foundation.

With this thrust toward having scientists, researchers, mathematicians, and inventors become more collaborative and share information, hypotheses, and results, we can look for more happy accidents that will improve our lives. In what ways . . . who knows? But the results will come out of a mix of technology and people—being cooperative and collaborative rather than insular and territorial.

You Never Know It Alls who experience serial serendipity generate these opportunities by being open, seeing the possibilities, and exhibiting the eight counterintuitive traits that contribute to their success. They seize the serendipity of the happy accident and turn it into something useful—or even delicious.

FRENCH SERENDIPITY SANDWICH

The *Los Angeles Times* reported on the ninety-fifth anniversary of the French dipped sandwich, whose invention was prompted ostensibly by an irate customer.[4]

Phillippe Matthieu of Aix en Provence moved to Los Angeles in 1903 and opened a French deli, and by 1918 he had opened a small restaurant deli in the industrial area. One Monday a firefighter from a local fire station came in and ordered a sandwich. Because the roll was left over from the weekend, it was stale. He walked into the kitchen to complain and saw some gravy in a pan of roast beef and asked if he could dip the roll in it! Five or six firemen saw what he did and also asked for the gravy. According to his grandson, Phillippe Guillome, Matthieu recognized a good idea and the positive customer response. The next day he made a gallon of gravy. And so the customer complaint begat a famous sandwich that appears on restaurant menus around the country: the French dipped roast beef sandwich.

The family sold the restaurant to its present owner, and "Phillippe's—the Original French Dipped Sandwich" has celebrated its ninety-fifth anniversary. That's longevity and success in the restaurant—or in any—business.

But there is more to this story than just serendipity. Phillippe Matthieu took action. He accommodated a customer by agreeing to let him dip his roll in a gravy pan. He also allowed five of his friends to do the same. And he "heard" the message from the market, observed his customers' satisfaction with the gravy-dipped rolls, and prepared a gallon of gravy the very next day. He listened to his customers—they were a very reliable "focus group."

Had Matthieu been enraged at the firefighter's visit to his kitchen, scoffed at the customer's request, and ignored the firemen's appreciation of the "happy accident," his business may not have been the long-running success it has turned out to be. Talk about riding the gravy train! The firemen helped Matthieu solve the problem of stale but perfectly edible (once soaked in gravy) rolls.

Sometimes a car accident turns into more than a collision . . .

YOU "AUTO" COLLABORATE

Being rear-ended after a long day of work was not what Leigh Bohmfalk had planned for her day. "I felt the bump before I heard her car hit mine," she reports. "Just what I needed! Rather than get upset, I got out of the car and checked the damage. It was visible but really didn't look horrible. At first the other driver claimed nothing had happened to my car, in a tone that was almost abrasive, but I stayed calm and politely pointed out the damage to her. I actually think my politeness took her by surprise. We exchanged information and went on our way.

"Once I got home I looked at the bumper again and decided not to report to the insurance, etc., because the damage wasn't too bad. There was a lot going on in my life, including a job search, and I just didn't want to put my energy into the accident.

"After I left her a message letting her know of my decision, she left me a very, very nice voice mail saying how much she appreciated my kindness, and that she was going through a lot because her parents were ill. She was also in the midst of a job search. She said she wanted to give me a bottle of wine as a thank-you gesture. I sent her an e-mail letting her know that it wasn't necessary and that I understood the pressure because I was also looking for work. I received an e-mail back from her with a piece of priceless information. In it she told me about the KITLIST, which is an amazing job resource list that I have been using since. It was a payoff for being polite to someone who didn't intend to hit my car. That is why they are called car 'accidents.'

Leigh's low-keyed response turned this inconvenient and "slightly" damaging accident into a serendipitous meeting with someone who ended up helping her in her job search. Nobody was hurt, no one had their insurance rates increased, and job leads were exchanged. What started as an unpleasant incident was a happy accident after all.

"Happy accidents" involve discoveries of one sort or another. They can also involve coincidences that may be plausible but statistically seem improbable.

KNOPF THREE TIMES: AN EPIC FANTASY

Christopher Paolini, a teenager, has a three-book deal with a venerable publisher, Alfred A. Knopf. In and of itself, this is good news but not a remarkable fact. *How* it happened is remarkable and involves an incredible set of circumstances and serendipity. The saga is almost too unbelievable to be fact—and it has turned this 19-year-old first-time author (who wrote his best seller when he was 15 into a literary phenom who is on the *New York Times* best seller list.

How I even know about it is another one of those "meant to be" moments. I happened to turn on the *Today* show while taking a coffee break from writing this chapter when I heard Katie Couric introduce Carl Hiassen and the young author he had "discovered." The story has since appeared in newspapers around the country. How Hiassen discovered Christopher's book is sweet serendipity.

While on a fishing trip to Montana, Hiassen and his wife visited a small, local bookstore because she was looking for an interesting book for the car trip for her 11-year-old son. She found *Eragon,* written and illustrated by Christopher Paolini, on a table, and it looked so interesting that she bought it. Hiassen told Katie Couric that there was not a sound out of the boy as they drove for over an hour. The book was so absorbing that his stepson claimed it "was better than Harry Potter." That claim certainly captured the attention of Hiassen, himself a best-selling author.

After thumbing through the book, Hiassen called his editor at Knopf and suggested he take a look at this little-known, self-published book. And his editor did. The result: Knopf purchased *Eragon,* and Christopher, at the ripe old age of 19, has a three-book deal.

The backstory is that when Christopher, who was homeschooled, finished his 528-page manuscript, he showed it to his parents, who own a small publishing house. The family decided to get behind the book and make publishing it a family affair and a commitment. It was published in hardback with an eye-catching cover.

Christopher spent a year promoting the book, giving 35 presentations around the country while wearing a medieval costume, which created some buzz and garnered attention. That it was in the Livingston, Montana, bookstore and that Carl Hiassen and his wife just happened to go into that store and browse is a coincidence. That Hiassen called his editor about the book is another special circumstance. He could have just been thrilled that his stepson was quietly reading on the car trip and not shown an interest in what the boy was reading. That he was so impressed that he picked up the phone and called his agent is mentorship at its finest.

Christopher did contribute to the success of this series of serendipitous situations because he is talented and honed his writing skills during his homeschooling. His parents did not publish an amateur piece of dreck—he had produced a fine, polished book with an attractive cover. They put out a top-quality product and they knew how to get his book the exposure it needed to reach even a small bookstore in Livingston, Montana. The result was that *Eragon* spent many weeks on the *New York Times* best seller list.

This saga of serendipity included a series of events that led to Christopher's very polished interview on the *Today* show with his mentor of sorts, Carl Hiassen, an old friend of Katie Couric's, from their days of working together in the Miami media.

Who could have predicted that a small bookstore in Livingston, Montana, would be the venue for such a discovery? Never assume, and never overlook the possibilities . . .

FALLING OFF THE TURKEY TRUCK

Some accidents initially aren't very happy at all. Just such an accident presented a problem that was resolved in an unusually proactive way.

Paul Caldarazzo had worked behind the seafood counter at Mollie Stone's, an independent supermarket chain, for over two decades. I hadn't seen him for a while when I bumped into him outside the market. He was wearing a white shirt and tie, and that was unusual. I asked him where he'd been and what was going on.

"This tie and get-up are what I wear for my new job," he replied. "I still work for Mollie Stone's, but no longer behind the counter."

Paul, a father of two, always had his day job, and his nights were devoted to rehearsals and gigs with his band, 35R. He continues, "This wasn't a change I had planned because we're cutting a new CD and were just under new management. All of this was going on and we were in our really busy season at Mollie Stone's—Thanksgiving. The delivery truck pulled in and there I was, unloading the 'merchandise' to try to find a turkey for a customer. Yes, I actually *fell off the turkey truck!* I broke my right wrist and left thumb and had quite a bump on my head. But there was no way I could do the counter work, filet the fish, cut up the chicken, or butcher the meat. But after over two decades, I knew a lot of meat and seafood purveyors and had been working with them for years and had been doing my present job on a part-time basis.

"I was really happy managing the department, working the counter, and working with our vendors for the other part of the time. I wanted to get back to work, not just stay at home and wait till I got well enough to 'filet fish.' I asked the owners what else I could do, and they made me the full-time merchandiser."

Paul's promotion was a result of a painful and, according to him, embarrassing accident. Had Paul not been a valued employee, had he not developed relationships with the vendors, and had he not fallen off the turkey truck, he would not have accelerated the appointment to his new full-time job.

Had he not fallen off the turkey truck, been injured, and become so bored that he wanted to get back to work,

Paul would not have asked about opportunities. Could it be that Paul was meant to be the meat and seafood merchandiser of Mollie Stone's? Probably. Was his fall off the turkey truck meant to be? Maybe. Maybe not.

Paul comments, "I really enjoy what I'm doing now and I also play with my band. Instead of working a counter, I spend more time in the car and in the office. The new position is great. But spending a lot of time in the car is different for me. I knew I was doing it more than I should when I tried to open my office door with the car key!"

Some accidents that were initially inconvenient, painful, and disruptive yield results that are positive. In Paul's case, falling off the turkey truck allowed him to fall into a new full-time job.

A NEW 24/7 CAREER

Success means different things to different people. Marcy McKay sees her success in the faces of her son and daughter, who she now has indirectly due to a happy accident that ended up being the result of good timing and some pertinent information from a former boss.

"On March 6, 2002," she relates, "my husband and I were matched by our adoption agency with a beautiful, six-week-old baby boy. I was at work when the call came, so my colleagues were some of the first to know the good news! At the time, my husband and I thought we had been through a lot in order to get to that day, but what we were about to experience proved far more difficult—and far more glorious—than anything we could have imagined.

"When we started the adoption process, we were told to expect a four- to six-month wait after 'the match' for our child to arrive from Guatemala. That timeline was quickly revised to a six- to nine-month wait, which was difficult to believe and even harder to reconcile emotionally. By September, however, things had taken a very bad turn, and we learned that our son would not be home for many more months.

"Terry, a former boss, who knew that we were adopting from Guatemala, connected me with a friend who had both professional and personal ties there. My ex-boss thought her friend Judy might be a good resource for me so I could learn more about the country. I got in touch with Judy, who put me in contact with Desiree, a business associate of hers, who had adopted from Guatemala. Before meeting Desiree, I had never heard of adoptive parents fostering their children while they waited, but the idea intrigued me. I tucked the idea away and waited.

"By October, I was making plans to move to Guatemala to foster-parent my son. Desiree was one of the first people I contacted. She put me in contact with Marjorie, a Guatemalan woman she had met, who was happy to help me in any way she could.

"A few days before I traveled, I e-mailed Marjorie a note to ask if we could meet when I arrived. I flew out November 4, and the next morning I had my son. It wasn't long before I learned that she had a friend who owned an orphanage. Upon hearing this, I immediately asked if I could meet the woman. My husband, Jeff, and I planned to adopt again, and I would need to explore all options, since we very clearly would not be using our current agency again. Marjorie was happy to oblige and set up a date for me to meet Sarita. As 'fate' would have it, I had to cancel that meeting because my son was sick, so we rescheduled for a week and a half later.

"On the day of our rescheduled appointment, December 5, Marjorie took me to meet Sarita and to see the children's home. When we got to the infant room, Sarita and Marjorie began to talk excitedly in Spanish, when Sarita picked up a beautiful *seven*-day-old baby girl and handed her to me. She told me that if I wanted to adopt her, I could. My dreams were coming true in ways I had never imagined!"

Marcy's You Never Know! experience truly had an element of coincidental timing that is almost eerie. Had her son not been sick and had she been able to keep the original appointment at the orphanage *ten* days earlier, the baby girl would not have been born.

"I knew the moment I held her that I was meant to be her mother, and I said yes. I called my husband to tell him that my visit to the orphanage meant that we also had a daughter!

"My lesson is that I have learned to be open to the people who come into my life and to be open to possibility. People have been put into my life for very specific purposes. I am the happiest person I know."

Marcy's happy accident resulted in a new and much sought-after 24/7 career—that of mom. She had a first career as, and still is, a writer. But now she has so much more material for her writing.

If we think of quality of life as an achievement, Marcy turned her You Never Know! experience into a most wonderful and heartwarming success. She was open about her and her husband's adoption plans and received good information from others about the process. She made a courageous decision to take a leave in order to move to Guatemala. Marcy followed up on all the leads and advice she received. That a former boss provided several contacts showed the quality of Marcy's work relationships and that she maintained them. She overcame her fear of moving to another country, when she did not speak the language, to become a foster parent for her son, and she took risks to achieve her goal.

Marcy happened to "accidentally" be at the orphanage at the right time. Had she been there 10 days earlier for the original appointment, her daughter would not have been born. Marcy, a woman of faith, believed it was a sign—that it was meant to be. Her will and **actions** should not be underestimated.

What can happen when we make decisions and leave our comfort zone? Anything. Everything.

THE WAITING GAME

On the Broadway stage there is a world of understudies who wait for their chance should the lead get sick or have an accident. The show must go on but not necessarily with the original cast. Lainie Kazan, now known for her starring role in the wildly successful film *My Big Fat Greek Wedding*, caught her break as the understudy for Barbra Streisand in the Broadway production of *Funny Girl*. Likewise, Ruthe Hirsch was the "understudy" of sorts who benefited from a happy accident that resulted in a dream career that came true.

ALL THE WORLD'S A STAGE

Ruthe Hirsch was the marketing consultant for a beautiful upscale restaurant and banquet facility in San Francisco in the late 1980s. As she tells it, "One day, I was contacted by a gentleman—for purposes of this story, I will call him 'Jim'—whom I had known from business, and I was aware that he was a fine singer. He wanted to bring his musical performance to the restaurant. I introduced him to the general manager, and the three of us met to determine how to implement this program. After receiving the manager's approval, I agreed to begin marketing a tour package to potential groups that would include a lunch and cabaret revue that Jim would write and direct. He would also be the star performer. His cast would include a pianist, a violinist, and a female soloist. My role was to sell his program and bring in the audience.

"Because of my background in music, I had the opportunity to do something I always wanted to do: perform a solo number. But Jim was not interested in anyone else's ideas or feedback. He was someone who had to control everything and was not an easy person.

"In the early 1990s the restaurant closed. We found a new restaurant location, and I promptly started to market our tour package and successfully booked groups for the entire year. But in February 1992, Jim had a fall in his home that resulted in a broken jaw (which was wired shut for several months), serious surgery, and a recuperative period of almost four years.

"When I was notified about his accident, my initial reaction was that of concern for Jim. Then panic set in when I realized that we were fully booked for the year and that Jim, who was the star, would no longer be able to perform. This was terrifying. I didn't know whether to do a mass cancellation or find another alternative. But marketing the shows was my livelihood and canceling them would have been very costly.

"I decided not to act hastily and to give it some serious thought. Then I remembered a man that I had met the previous year when I sang and competed in the Ms. Senior America Pageant. He had accompanied me on the piano, played the trumpet, and had an impressive musical background, and he knew I could sing and perform. I contacted him and invited him to join the cast. I rewrote, produced, and directed the show as I had always envisioned it. It was something I could not do as long as Jim was the star and at the helm. I realized that I finally had the opportunity of doing the show my way.

"Each year, I write a new cabaret revue and we continue to welcome the new and returning groups and always delight in receiving standing ovations. Each time we take the stage I am so happy that I didn't send that mass cancellation letter."

Jim's unfortunate accident was not something Ruthe Hirsch wanted to have happen. But it did, as accidents do occur. She seriously assessed the options and made some hard decisions to salvage the show. By doing so, she set the stage for realizing her dream of performing. But that was not all she did. Ruthe had a lot of work to do. She had to find other cast members; transition the troupe; write, produce, direct, and perform—and help book the audiences.

"It's a lot of work . . . and I've never been happier!" she proclaims.

Sometimes the serendipity of an unhappy accident—along with a lot of hard work, energy, and time—turns into a success.

ANOTHER PURPOSE FOR AN INFAMOUS PILL

Under the umbrella of multiple uses, scientists are now doing research that could affect millions of people who suffer from altitude sickness. That cure might just be . . . Viagra. No kidding. In *USA Today*, Daniel Baer reports that researchers in the United Kingdom are testing the drug as a cure for altitude sickness, which occurs, as does impotence, when blood vessels are too constricted.[5] The researchers hope that Viagra will aid the transfer of oxygen from the lungs to the bloodstream. The research is sponsored by Apex, the British medical charity. Should this experiment with Viagra work, the drug could also be used to treat asthma.

An expedition to Bolivia, where there is a physics lab at an altitude of 17,060 feet, is part of the experiment. The participants are premed students and interns ranging in age from 18 to 24. Researchers hope to show that "Viagra will make athletic activity at high altitudes easier." Another "happy" accident for sports enthusiasts.

When we look at how products, medicines, and other discoveries were made, we recognize that many were the result of an accident that turned out to be serendipitous and very beneficial. Our grade school geography studies provided lessons of explorers who set out on journeys that had unpredictable endings because they didn't find what they expected. Much like Christopher Columbus, they made discoveries that yielded unexpected bonuses.

What we can learn from the scientists, as well as from the people with new jobs, new careers, or even new families, is that opportunities can emerge out of incidents and accidents. We just need to be more open and aware.

RoAne's Reminders

- **Ask** for help, ideas, or more job responsibilities. People will not assume you are interested unless you make it known that you are. *If* Paul had not asked his boss what else he could do, he would not have been given his current full-time job to replace the part-time one.
- **Analyze** current situations, options, and possible solutions to difficult issues.
- **Listen** to the marketplace as well as observe and overhear. *If* a customer, colleague, or friend is interested in

a solution, product, or service (such as soaking up gravy to make day-old rolls softer), pay attention.

- **Give information** to get more back. It may seem like small talk but the more you share, the more likely you are to receive additional information. The exchange of information, ideas, and advice fuels the You Never Know It Alls.
- **Act** on good advice and information to turn the opportunity or coincidence into success.
- **Build good relationships** with colleagues, bosses, vendors, and competitors.
- **Be open** to surprises, discoveries, and unintended conclusions.

There are people all around us to whom things have happened that were unplanned, unexpected, and unwanted—they happened by "accident." But some of these "accidents" are disguised opportunities. It's a case-by-case call.

How to Become More "Accident Prone"

The "Accident" (or Unlucky Event)	How You Responded	How You *Could* Have Responded	The Opportunity
1. _____	_____	_____	_____
2. _____	_____	_____	_____
3. _____	_____	_____	_____
4. _____	_____	_____	_____
5. _____	_____	_____	_____
6. _____	_____	_____	_____
7. _____	_____	_____	_____

If the "opportunity" in the accident (or unlucky event) evades you, invite some trusted friends and colleagues for a brain-trust session over a beverage of your choice. If two heads are better than one, then five heads are a bonanza.

WHO'D'A THUNK IT?

There are people whose lives are dramatically altered by circumstances they could never have imagined or planned. In each case, someone was able to convert a You Never Know! event—a coincidence, an accident, or even a mistake—into an opportunity or, for some, a series of them. Many of the stories in this book have an element of incredulity but for the You Never Know It Alls in this chapter, the results are more amazing.

Every day, each of us meets new people. Sometimes it's by accident, sometimes by means of an introduction. How many times do we fail to look beneath the surface and discover opportunities? The You Never Know! experiences shared in this book show that there are possibilities are all around us that are pleasantly surprising. To reiterate, what we have to do to create our own successful experience is to be open to those possibilities, see the potential opportunities, and **take the actions** that could turn serendipity into success.

Sometimes we dial the wrong number but end up talking to the right person.

RINGING THE WRONG NUMBER

Much to his surprise, Lee Ring dialed a wrong number and discovered that it could not have been more right. Lee now has partnered with a new associate and has a new e-book, the-Book.biz, available for purchase as a result of that call.

"I had meant to call one of my contacts at the Atlanta Board of Realtors," he says, "when I heard an unfamiliar voice at the other end of the call. I apologized for the interruption and immediately explained that I was trying to reach the Board of Realtors."

Lee had accidentally called a lawyer with an Atlanta law firm that specialized in labor and employment law—a field far removed from the real estate industry. Rather than hanging up, the attorney inquired about Lee's connection to the real estate industry. Ignoring their completely different backgrounds, both men were friendly and struck up a conversation.

Lee continues, "When I explained that I was involved in the real estate industry, the lawyer said that he had an interest in a company that was developing an e-book for real estate agents, but that he was just a 'silent partner' and knew nothing about real estate." The lawyer said the book was not complete, and the author wanted to sell his interest in the business. When he realized that Lee was not only involved in the real estate business but was also thoroughly familiar with the subject matter of the e-book, the lawyer asked Lee to review the marketing material and the e-book and meet for a drink after work when the review was complete.

"As soon as we met," Lee says, "the lawyer went over

my assessment and suggestions, and he realized that I would make the perfect partner to complete the book and market it. I arranged to meet with the author and negotiated an agreement to purchase the author's shares in the company. I completed the book and am now marketing it."

Who would have thought that a misdial would turn into a great opportunity? A lot of telephone calls turn out to be wrong numbers and are quickly concluded—sometimes with an apology, too often without one. Lee took the few extra seconds to explain whom he was trying to reach, and the attorney was gracious and intrigued enough to pick up on the conversation cue. Because of that and some old-fashioned good manners, this misdial resulted in successful deal.

Points to Ponder

What made this "who woulda thunk it" possible? The answer is simple, but one that most people ignore: Courtesy, friendliness, interest in other people, and effort made all the difference.

Lee gave additional information when he reached the wrong person rather than just apologize for the disturbance and hang up. The attorney built on that information, asking a question based on Lee's additional information. Both were polite, and each of them took the time to learn a little bit about the other, rather than simply terminating the accidental phone call with an "I'm sorry" and a "No problem."

Through their conversation, both Lee and the attorney were alert to an opportunity, no matter how unlikely. When they determined that there was possible mutual interest, Lee took the time to review the draft and think about what was necessary to complete it. Both men were quick to recognize a good "fit" and act on it.

As a result, they turned a wrong number into a thriving business opportunity.

Some days, the ticket to success is not what we thought it would be.

PARKING TICKET "SALE"

Like Alan Postle, some of us have had a You Never know! story on a slightly different theme. Alan explains, "I was illegally parked in an alley right beside the backstop of a playing field where my team was scheduled to play. I had all the softball equipment (bat bag, bases, balls, etc.), and the parking lot was way off beyond the left field fence. Not wanting to carry all the stuff that distance, I parked as close to home plate as I could, unloaded the equipment, and began setting up the bases as my teammates began to arrive. Just then, a commissionaire (police officer) came along and began writing me out a parking ticket. I jumped over the fence and hurried to my car.

"The officer seemed friendly enough, so I pleaded with him and explained my predicament. I showed him all the bags that I had to carry, pointed out to him how far away the parking lot was, gave him my best puppy-dog look, and hoped for the best. To my surprise and delight, he tore up the ticket, giving me some good-natured ribbing, and suggested that next time I get my teammates to help me carry everything. I replied in a loud voice—so my mates could hear—that I wouldn't expect much help from those lazy bums. During the playful insults and jesting that ensued between myself and my teammates and the officer, I managed to give my business card to him.

"Several months later, this commissionaire got in touch with me. He ended up buying a new fifth-wheel trailer from me. Somehow, I managed to avoid a costly parking ticket and turn it into a nice, fat sales commission."

Who would have thought that being pleasant and good-natured in the midst of a potentially painful situation might work itself out so well? You just never know! Had Alan been overbearing, belligerent, or overtly negative, he would have gotten the ticket instead of the sale.

Alan sees opportunities and possibility in both painful and pleasant situations. As a matter of course, he gives out his card so that people know he's "legit"—a business-man in the community. Because of his demeanor and serendipity, he earned a successful sale.

For some, the path to a career or business is the result of a painful set of situations.

PERSONAL IMAGE SUCCESS

The old expression "dressed to the nines" perfectly describes Diane Parente, an award-winning image consultant, founder and first president of the Association of Image Consultants International, and author of four books. No matter what the occasion, even on an aerobic walk, she looks fabulous. I sure don't look glamorous on my aerobic walks.

She has "dressed" corporate executives, society ladies, and entrepreneurs, all of whom benefit from her innate sense of style. One day, as she was analyzing my dress for my "milestone birthday party," I watched her look at me and scrutinize the color, the fit, the design of my gown.

When she finally spoke, she told me that the sleeves on the jacket needed to be tapered, as they made me look boxy and short. At 4 feet 11 inches, I don't need to look any shorter and certainly not boxy. She took a few straight pins, worked her magic, and—voila!—she transformed my wonderful red gown. What an eye!

"Diane, you must have been born with a *Vogue* magazine in your hand because you have such amazing sense of style!" I exclaimed.

"What you see now is very different from what I was like," she responded. "At 14, I learned the very hard way about image and dress, and the lessons were so painful. In my first year of high school, I was the butt of everyone's jokes because of the way I dressed. My dad had died and my mother worked as a waitress to support us. There was no extra money for cashmere sweater sets with skirts to match. Not only were my clothes uncool, they were very inexpensive and had no style. They became the reason I was ridiculed.

"That first year of high school was torture. I was quiet, shy, and a real loner. I was on the outside looking in. I spent the time observing the different groups in my high school. They called me Olive Oyl because I was tall and skinny and my feelings were in a perpetual state of hurt."

Diane, who has a marvelous sense of humor, liked the people who were funny even then because they were also smart and never judgmental or cruel. "I knew I was fun and could be funny and that part of me so wanted to belong," she comments. "But I knew that the opinions were already made and that I was 'out.'

"Fortunately, we moved that summer and I was going to start Novato High in September. I knew what I had to do . . . and that was to dress in such a way that I would be given a chance. My mother knew how to sew, so I asked if she would help me. We went to the fabric store and bought the patterns of the clothes I had seen and liked. Fabric was on sale for 29 cents a yard—which we could afford.

"It worked. I walked onto the campus the first day and was greeted by the group of kids I wanted to hang out with. It was then that I learned that if you create the image you want and dress the part, it opens doors . . . especially to friendships. They accepted me for what I looked like and that allowed me to express who I am. I was invited into clubs and asked to be a song leader. The last three years of high school were so different from the first one.

"Never in a million years could I have predicted that my horrible first year in high school would lead to where I am now and what I do. I later worked in a boutique and my boss took me to the fashion shows in New York. I learned the retail business, how to serve the customers, and how to help them find their image and style. My boss even had me 'dress' the windows.

"Then one day, one of our customers, a medical doctor with a busy practice and a family, came up to me after she had seen the window displays I designed. 'You're so good at putting things together and I have such a tough time with it, would you help me with my clothes?' Bingo! I heard her loudly and clearly."

Diane had the good fortune to receive a request from the marketplace that she heeded. It was kismet, serendipity, or simply "meant to be" to be asked to work with her first private client. Because she was taking business classes and wanted to start her own business, Diane paid attention to what the "doctor prescribed." In addition to her private image and wardrobe consulting, she shares her expertise with corporate and convention audiences as well as community organizations that help women in transition.

Who would have thought that teenage trauma and taunts would turn into Diane Parente's personal passion and image-building business? While she says she "found her business," in some ways her business found her.

Sometimes taking a good look at our lives and asking questions that challenge us become life-changing, and we, in turn, help challenge and change others.

AN UNCOMMON ATHLETE

David Miln Smith, known as King of the Risk Takers, teaches team building in the corporate world and was an innovator in the world of extreme sports and wilderness therapy. But as a young man he was known for his wild parties, his obsession with golf, and hanging out at the bar he owned, which was the watering hole for the in crowd. He was living life in the fast lane and seemed to love every minute of it.

"One day I was sitting in my car with my girlfriend, taking in the magnificent scenic view area of the Golden Gate Bridge," David remembers, "when I told her that I had to make some changes in my life. Rather than just accept my sweeping generalization, Judy was smart enough to ask me what I meant by my comment. I told her that there must be more to life than parties, golf, and making money but that I had no idea how to proceed.

"To her credit, she asked if there was something I always wanted to do, but had not. As I stared at the swirling waters of the bay, I realized that I always wanted to swim the gate, pointing down to the waters under the Golden Gate Bridge. When she mentioned that to swim across to the other shore you have to be in good physical condition, I realized that was why I'd never done it. Drinking and swimming don't mix well. And you really have to train for that swim. Judy looked me in the eye and said, 'You can do it.'

"I heard her words as a great challenge and an even greater source of support and started the work to convert my out-of-shape, overweight, three-pack-a-day smoker, and nightly drinker's body into one fit enough to swim the gate. And I did. From there I trained and became a world-record-breaking swimmer and the first person to swim from Africa to Europe. My life's work changed, and it became one of showing, by example, that we don't have to compete with anyone but ourselves to have an athletic experience.

"Many athletic endeavors don't need uniforms, teams, stadiums, ballparks, or arenas in order for us to be a participant. At the time this concept was either unknown or unpopular and seemingly against all we were taught about sports—'it's all about competition' and 'winning isn't everything, it's the only thing.' I was attempting to make a link between good health (not just the lack of disease) and a quality of life that included a fitness experience. Once fit, we can participate in a variety of athletic disciplines."

David created and was the sole participant in the first multisport event called the Peace Pentathlon, which landed him on the cover of *Sports Illustrated*—beating out Mario Andretti for the honor. Among his adventures, he has kayaked the Nile and part of the Amazon, climbed Mt. Sinai, and run a solo marathon in the Sahara Desert. He continues to motivate, educate, and inspire others to perform extraordinary feats in their everyday lives. As an author, David Miln Smith shares his message through his books and speeches. He is an uncommon athlete who chose to live an extraordinary life.

We never know when a question, asked at the right time, in the right way, will ignite a fire within and change a life. But there is no magic. David knew he wanted change in his life—and he made it happen. He did the training and the work, investigated the adventures, applied the skills he learned as an Eagle Scout as he researched the venues and planned a major event, the Extreme Challenge across the world. It became his life's work. He attracted interest, sponsors, and publishers, and for several years was Johnny Carson's guest adventurer, sharing his exploits with late-night audiences on *The Tonight Show.* Who would have thought that this former playboy would create NBC's *Survival of the Fittest* and go on to lead an unparalleled life of adventure that he turned into his career and life's work? Not David Miln Smith.

Some people develop an expertise that was never planned.

OVERLAPPING CIRCLES OF SERENDIPITY

Jon Tandler is an expert in copyright, publishing, and software law, and is a shareholder of Isaacson, Rosenbaum, Woods & Levy in Denver, Colorado. He is a faculty member of the University of Denver Publishing Institute, lectures nationally in his field, and has a full corporate practice with a parallel niche in publishing. Did he plan this? He did not. Because of serendipity, kismet, timing, and wonderful mentoring by more senior attorneys, Jon's career had an interesting genealogy that he can trace.

"In 1988, when I was working in San Francisco, our senior partner, William (Bill) Coblentz, a highly regarded lawyer and business leader, took me to lunch with the creators and publishers of the acclaimed A Day in the Life® series of photojournalism books. The publishing company had just moved from New York to San Francisco, and needed local counsel. Bill and their New York–based lawyer, E. Gabriel Perle, both attended Yale Law School and remained friends over the years. Gabe called Bill, who had me do the work, and I was introduced to publishing.

"Gabe Perle is a preeminent authority on copyright and publishing law. He started his publishing career in Time Inc.'s legal department, ultimately serving as its general counsel in charge of the company's legal affairs. He served on the national campaign which determined and recommended the computer software and certain other new technological works to be afforded copyright protection, has testified before Congress on significant copyright legislation, is coauthor of *Perle & Williams on Publishing Law* (Aspen, 1999), and is senior counsel of his Stamford, Connecticut, law firm. Gabe has been a teacher, mentor, and close friend to me since I met him in 1988.

"Two years later, in 1990, I received a call from John Kilcullen, also referred by Gabe. John was the publisher and soon-to-be president and CEO of IDG Books Worldwide, the newly formed book publishing subsidiary of International Data Group, the computer magazine conglomerate. IDG Books was based in Silicon Valley, had three employees at the time, and engaged our firm as publishing counsel. John and IDG Books created the very successful For Dummies® brand of technology and trade books, and developed and acquired several other well-known consumer brands. John and his team grew IDG Books into a large company, and I was able to learn and grow with it.

"In 1994, I contacted the director of the Stanford University Summer Publishing Course in Palo Alto, to see if I could teach an electronic media law course there. I had never taught any legal subject before, and although it took a little convincing, she agreed to my class. I ultimately lectured there from 1994 to 1997. In 1996, after my late afternoon class, I had a glass of wine—which I rarely did—in the faculty area with another instructor, a successful San Francisco book publisher. We discussed the books his company published and my law practice.

"A few months later, I received a call from Michael Reagan, an experienced and respected publisher and book packager in Atlanta. My friend and fellow instructor from the Stanford Course referred Michael to me. Michael's company, Lionheart Books, Ltd., needed representation on a unique and important project. In addition to being a wonderful client and friend today, Michael has referred significant other clients to me.

"Because I really enjoy teaching, when my wife and I moved to Denver with our children in 1996, I contacted Elizabeth Geiser, the founder and executive director of the University of Denver Publishing Institute, to see if I could teach its law course. Elizabeth couldn't use me that year, as the institute had been well served for years by the general counsel of a large New York publishing house. In 1997, however, due to a business emergency, he could not come to Denver for his scheduled lecture. Having just heard from him, Elizabeth called me on a Saturday afternoon to see if I could teach the three-hour class on the following Friday. Even though it was short notice, how could I say no? Timing is timing. July 2004 was my seventh year on the faculty. My teaching experience as well as being part of the institute are invaluable to me.

"My work has led me to other important professional affiliations, including the Copyright Society of the United States, lecturing at the New York University Summer Publishing Institute, and teaching at Colorado Independent Publishers Association (CIPA) programs. Through my activities, I have made lasting friendships, learned much from others, and established important career relationships."

Jon Tandler never planned a legal practice in publishing, but was **open** to the opportunities that Gabe Perle and others have provided. He does the work, follows through, and performs so well for his clients that they are all too happy to share his name with others. He makes sure that each person is properly acknowledged so that they know he appreciates their support and referrals.

Jon follows where the leads lead him and stays in touch with his network on paper, on the phone, over the Internet, and over a beverage or meal. He allocates the time to attend the professional society meetings and has maintained visibility. When he was asked to teach on very short notice, Jon could have said no, but he said yes—as You Never Know It Alls do. Because he experienced an overlapping series of serendipity that he seized, Jon Tandler developed his successful career, his law practice, and his unplanned parallel niche in publishing.

Sometimes a planned business meeting has an unplanned—and successful—result.

"LOVE AT FIRST SITE" INSPECTION

As people who are involved in any aspect of event planning know, site inspections are key to venue selection. This applies to anyone looking for just the right place for a convention, retreat, family reunion, party, or wedding.

Jo Ann Worthington was working as a sales manager at the Los Angeles Convention and Visitors Bureau with a client who was not interested in booking the Convention Center. "The client was very specific," she says. "They wanted a venue that was tiered, not flat. I was determined to find the right venue, as booking the client's convention depended on it. The legendary Shrine Auditorium came to mind. So I called the general manager and made an appointment to do the preliminary site inspection."

It turned into a "sight" inspection as well. As the Shrine Auditorium general manager tells it, the minute Jo Ann walked in for their meeting, it was "love at first sight" for

Jo Ann and him. The Shrine Auditorium got two bookings out of the meeting. The first was the convention that Jo Ann was able to book because it was a tiered venue. And the second event was their wedding reception, on the stage of the splendid Shrine Auditorium, featuring their tiered wedding cake.

Jo Ann was just doing her job, trying to meet the needs of her client. She was prepared for the appointment and dressed for a meeting. She is a charming, energetic, positive, and knowledgeable person who is now the vice president of sales at LA Inc, the Convention and Visitors Bureau, and her husband of a dozen years is still enjoying his position as general manager of the Shrine Auditorium. When serendipity is in play, the benefits of business can blossom beyond the bottom line. According to Jo Ann, "In Los Angeles, anything is possible. You never know what is around the proverbial corner."

Sometimes a personal career need becomes a worldwide winner.

INTERNATIONAL NETWORKING

Dr. Ivan Misner is the founder of BNI (Business Networking International), with over 3,000 chapters in 16 countries. "I was teaching at Cal State Pomona and was also a management consultant specializing in organizational behavior, dealing with policies and manuals," he says. "In 1985, my biggest client had financial reversals and did not renew my contract. The timing of such things is never good—but for me, it was awful, as we had just bought a new home with a rather large mortgage.

"I really had to rethink my business and come up with a solution to restructure my business. Clients always come to me via referrals, so that seemed to be an area of focus for my efforts. So I invited some colleagues and associates I trusted and respected to meet and share my situation. We brainstormed, shared referrals, and the idea for BNI was formulated. I wish I could tell you that I had a vision of BNI as the global enterprise it has now become, but the truth was, I was just trying to rebuild my business for the sake of my mortgage.

"There were other lead-generating groups formed, but ours had a structure and an educational component. One thing we had over other structured networking groups was a positive approach. . . . We didn't fine people when they didn't bring referrals. Because we permit only one person per profession, a woman contacted me saying she wanted to be part of BNI, and wondered if I would help her start another group. And then another person called and asked for help with a BNI chapter, and another . . .

"Networking is so important to business and to our lives in general. While some people are excellent at it and are naturals, others need a structured environment. We need to teach networking in our educational institutions. I started a class in networking at Cal Poly, Pomona, and continue to educate people in 16 countries as we spread the word.

"In 1985, I was teaching and I still am. But the audiences are global, older, and are helping others realize their dreams as they are realizing their own."

You never know how a need might turn into a deed, and a good idea, when it's organized by an organization consultant. And then it turns into an international success. Dr. Misner said yes to helping start a second, third, and fourth chapter of BNI. He was busy and could have said no.

By the way, Dr. Misner and his wife bought their dream home. You never know how things will turn out. Their house was directly on the path of the fires raging in Southern California in 2003, when the winds abruptly changed and their house was saved. "A firestorm does give one a new perspective on coincidence, timing, and you-never-know events," he comments.

Sometimes tenure can be tenuous.

EDUCATING THE EDUCATORS

More than two decades ago, Anne Miller, a former teacher, realized that many teachers wished they could be doing something else. "I had a sideline hobby where I taught teachers how to leave teaching and get into business," she explains. "Shortly after my programs started, school enrollments were decreasing and, for the first time in many years, teachers were being let go. This trend went against the promises of tenure and 'always having something to fall back on.' Thanks to the grapevine, word about my programs in New York City got out, and a writer for *Working Woman* magazine interviewed and quoted me in an article on the topic.

"Within two weeks of the magazine's publication date, 200 letters poured in from anguished teachers around the country, begging for personal advice. Since this was pre-Internet and pre-Google, and my address was not listed, they had to work hard to track me down to get their letters to me. That overwhelming—and totally unexpected—response told me that there was a huge need for such counseling around the country. I listened to the message from the market and subsequently wrote a book on the subject, *Finding Career Alternatives for Teachers* (Apple, 1979), and wound up running seminars for teachers all over the United States. I never would have gone that route if I hadn't received—and acted on—all that unexpected mail."

Anne Miller now works with corporations and is the author of *365 Sales Tips for Winning Customers* (Perigee, 1998), but 23 years ago she was one of the few people who focused on helping teachers. As a victim of the 1979 school district layoffs in San Francisco, which affected 1,200 teachers, I tracked down Anne a soon as I read about her. Her book was the resource for career change workshop attendees nationwide. Anne paid attention to the concerns and grumblings from dissatisfied teachers and designed a program to solve the problem. She worked hard, helped people, and garnered referrals. Who would have thought that Anne's career coaching for teachers would spark nationwide interest and take her business in a new direction?

To say Anne Miller was lucky does a disservice to her and negates the hours of research, assessments, module construction, and information sourcing she did to support and help teachers. The lesson that Anne shares with her current clients is this: "When we are aware of unexpected turns and twists that have happened in our world and that of our clients, we can identify the problems, exploit them, and offer solutions." Since then, Anne has built a widely respected sales and presentations consulting business. That is the serendipity of being open, taking in information, and seeing possibility and opportunity in the midst of a problem.

Some people never meant to, but end up taking the town by storm.

POINT, CLICK, AND LIST

Most people who use the Internet have heard of craigslist .org. Started in San Francisco by a shy programmer, Craig Newmark, it has evolved from an informal event list into one of the most heavily trafficked communities on the Web. It all started because Craig Newmark collected information about events happening in the San Francisco Bay Area, as well as job openings. According to *Investors Business Daily*,[1] he sent these e-mails out to his friends, and they got passed around. Because he was a programmer who could write code, he turned all of those e-mails into Web pages.

"Craigslist is the ultimate option for people seeking possibility," said Mary Haring, a frequent visitor. "Whether it's the possibility of a job or apartment or tickets to a concert or finding the person who wants to buy your car, there is the hope that your visit will solve a problem and present an opportunity. It's easy to use and doesn't have a ton of annoying ads. And everyone uses it. It's a great way of helping people find what they need and connect with each other. That's the essence of community," adds Mary.

Craig Newmark did not pitch a "great dot-com business" plan. He didn't seek venture capital and spend millions of other people's dollars on a "swift" idea. Oddly enough, the man who just tried to help friends stay in the loop is the founder of a successful, growing company that is currently in 25 cities and is expanding into Canada, the United Kingdom, New Zealand, and Australia.

Most of the dot-com venture capital–backed businesses have disappeared, but craigslist is growing exponentially. Who would have thought that a desire to help friends and keep them posted would turn into an enterprise that provides possibilities for millions of people?

One may not always be the loneliest number.

BECOMING A CATEGORY OF ONE

Joe Calloway, a professional speaker and restaurateur, is the author of *Becoming a Category of One* (Wiley, 2003). But his life contained no such accomplishments 20-some years ago. As he tells it, "In Nashville, Tennessee, in the summer of 1982 I was struggling (as in, how do I pay the rent this month?) with the start-up of my new sales training business. I'd get a small job here and there, but it was very slow going. All I knew to do was (1) do good work for the very few clients I had, and (2) put myself in the path of opportunity as often as possible.

"After doing a sales training session for a local company, one of the participants said that I should call on the real estate company where her husband worked because they might need some sales training. Having plenty of time on my hands (translation: practically no work!), I had the luxury of being able to follow up on that sort of "opportune possibility," so I called her husband and asked him to lunch. When I went by his office to pick him up, he was talking with a fellow agent, and I asked her to join us.

"Turns out that there seemed to be little opportunity for training at the real estate firm, but his friend suggested that I call on her husband, Earl, who was the director of training for a local bank. A few days later I called on Earl, who I thought was a great guy but who currently had no work for me because all of their outside sales training was being done by someone else. But Earl invited me to stop by and say hello anytime.

"About three months later I found myself in the office building of Earl's bank to call on another prospect. I remembered his invitation, so I stopped by Earl's office and he was on the phone. I gestured that I was just saying 'hi' and was ready to leave, but Earl waved me in and pointed to the chair. It was truly a case of being in the right place at the right time . . . coincidentally so.

"He hung up the phone and asked me if I could start doing sales training for all of their locations around the state beginning the next week. I was stunned and very happy but felt I had to ask about what had happened to their sales trainer.

" 'He died day before yesterday,' Earl said.

"Believe me, that was not the answer I expected, but I said that I was sorry it happened and followed that with, 'And, yes, I can start next week.'

"It was all because I put myself in the path of people who knew people who knew people. Luck? I don't think so. Opportunity happens. We just have to show up."

Joe also followed up each lead he was given and took the time to meet each person. He included someone in a lunch invitation who just happened to be in the real estate office. Although that would increase his tab, Joe felt it would also increase his contacts. He established rapport and a relationship so that each person led him to another one. He followed through on Earl's open-ended invitation. The serendipitous timing of that visit was a turning point for Joe's business, which also grew because he worked hard and served each of his sales training clients. Joe Calloway is an in-demand keynote speaker who is well thought of by his clients and colleagues and has become a category of one.

Sometimes a dream of "crossing the pond" can come true.

STREETS PAVED WITH GOLD-EN OPPORTUNITIES

Who would have imagined that a 21-year-old hairdresser from Wimborne in Dorset, England, would become one of the most highly acclaimed professional speakers and speech coaches in America? Surely not Patricia Fripp.

"I became a hairdresser at 15 and was happily working at my craft when my best friend and hero, Wendy Roberts, who was 18 and had a pen pal in America, said we should go there," Patricia recalls. "When I was ready to travel, Wendy had just become engaged to a school chum of mine. Instead, I went to the Island of Jersey, off the coast, to work. When my pals there asked where we should next go to work and mentioned Spain, I had my mind set on America.

"Talk about coincidence! I had only met six people who'd ever been to America and all of them said, 'You must go to San Francisco!' That made the decision of where to go very easy. Another friend decided she would go with me on my adventure.

"I went immediately to the American Embassy to get a visa. As I had a profession and could support myself, it was approved. Talk about timing! Ten days later the laws changed and my friend couldn't get a visa! Prior to leaving for America, one of my clients in the Channel Isles gave me the name and number of her daughter who lived in America. She is the one who gave me the name of four salons, and one was at the Mark Hopkins Hotel. Once I landed in San Francisco, I went to the salon at the Mark Hopkins Hotel and met Charles le Von, the salon manager. At the time, he had no job for me.

"But we got on quite well, and he jokingly told people I was his 'mail order British bride.' He was a mentor and became a very good friend who took me under his wing and to the beauty school so I could get an American license. I had already been in the hairstyling business for over five years and knew how to cut hair and work fast, and I always worked hard.

"After I received my license, Charles hired me to work at the Mark Hopkins Hotel salon." Because she wanted to build her clientele, Patricia gave presentations to local organizations and joined Toastmasters to improve her public speaking. She worked hard at the craft and became the star of her Dale Carnegie classes. Soon her clients were asking her to speak to their Rotary Clubs and staff meetings.

She continues, "Within 10 years, I had my own salon—for men—and was a male stylist. Some of my clients are still friends and now hire me to train their sales teams in public speaking. To learn more about speaking, I also joined the National Speakers Association and continued to cut hair and manage my salon as well as my nine employees. I continued to work at both my careers that have been the result of seeing opportunities and pursuing possibilities.

"Standing behind my barber's chairs for many years, I received an education from some brilliant businessmen that continues to serve me well today."

A series of You Never Know! experiences combined for an interesting career and life. None of this would have happened had Patricia not pursued a dream, followed up on opportunities in a timely fashion, sought out additional education to enhance her skills, and built relationships along the way. Patricia, who is no longer a barber, sold her shop over 10 years ago and has turned her professional speaking skills into an international speakers school and an executive speech coaching business.

And she still gives a great haircut to her most famous client, her brother, Robert Fripp, internationally known guitarist and founder of the rock band King Crimson.

Because we never know what's around the proverbial corner, we should take that walk around it and find out.

AN EMMY-AWARD-WINNING STORY

The way I learned Jo Ann Worthington's story is another example of serendipity. My friend Dan Maddux was the guest of the Los Angeles Convention and Visitors Bureau for a weekend that included tickets to the 2003 Emmy Awards. He had an extra ticket and invited me to fly to Los Angeles to join him. Jo Ann was his host and liaison from the Convention and Visitors Bureau.

I expected that my trip to the Emmys would be a fabulous experience, as I watch more television than most people I know. Jo Ann's You Never Know! story was a "small talk" conversation we had at the Emmys—and you read the results earlier in this chapter. I thought I would just be checking out the red carpet, seeing some of my favorite actors, and maybe getting to meet a few (which I did). A story for this book? Who woulda thunk it?

Most of the people in this chapter regard their current destinations as positive. But, like most of the people who shared their stories in this book, not one of them ever thought or planned or even dared to dream that their serendipity would turn into such success.

———————————————■———————————————

RoAne's Reminders

Each You Never Know It All did it differently, but what they have in common is that they

- **Pursued, persevered,** and **"listened"** to the market-place
- **Were open** and **responded** to possibilities
- **Exhibited one or more of the eight traits:** talked to strangers, made small talk, dropped names, asked for help and offered it, had gracious endings and exits, eavesdropped, strayed from a chosen path, said "yes" instead of "no"
- **Followed up** leads, ideas, and advice and picked up the phone
- **Allocated "face" time** for meetings (a lunch, a cup of coffee, or a drink)
- **Expected the unexpected** to be positive and that it would be something that would benefit their careers or business and personal lives

"You Never Know!"

If we look at the experiences described in this book, we see patterns. They are part of a process that invites possibilities into our daily lives. Furthermore, the patterns reflect actions and behaviors of the You Never Know It Alls that we can embrace. When we do, we can take what crosses our proverbial paths and create positive results in our professional and personal lives.

Whether we call it serendipity, luck, kismet, *que sera,* lagniappe, the *beshert,* or coincidence, these real-life stories are the experiences that offer hope as well as a helpful guideline.

It's my wish that you enjoyed meeting the people in this book and found them as inspiring, interesting, and engaging as I did.

I hope that you will invite opportunity into your life and take the steps needed to turn serendipity into your "You Never Know!" success and create your own luck.

—Susan RoAne

APPENDIX

THE 10 COMMANDMENTS FOR TURNING SERENDIPITY INTO SUCCESS

    I. Thou shalt pay attention and be **open** to opportunity.

   II. Thou shalt be approachable; smile and make eye contact with others.

 III. Thou shalt do good deeds; say kind words, as they are oft returned.

 IV. Thou shalt create a network of associates, colleagues, friends, family, and coworkers.

   V. Thou shalt **stay in touch** with thy network when thou **needest nothing** from it.

 VI. Thou shalt be a supportive Yeah! Sayer.

VII. Thou shalt not render prejudgments.

VIII. Thou shalt follow up the leads, ideas, and connections offered by thy network.

IX. Thou shalt be positive and look at the glass as half full.

X. Thou shalt embrace these **eight (counterintuitive) traits:**

> Talk to strangers.
> Make small talk.
> Drop names.
> Ask for and offer help.
> Stray from paths.
> Eavesdrop and listen.
> Exit graciously without burning bridges.
> Say yes instead of no to opportunities and requests.

YIDDISH GLOSSARY

The following are some of the Yiddish terms I've used in this book. There are others that are frequently used in magazines (*Men's Health, Entertainment Weekly, The New Yorker, Glamour, Fortune, The Economist*), newspapers (*The Wall Street Journal, The Dallas Morning News, San Francisco Chronicle, USA Today, The Washington Post*), and on television (*Today, Will and Grace, The Simpsons,* and many others). These definitions are modified from Leo Rosten's *The Joys of Yiddish* (McGraw-Hill, 1968). I've also added some expressions from our current lexicon that are known as "Yinglish."

Beshert   Fate. Meant to be or not meant to be. The "essence" of You Never Know!

> "It was *beshert* that we should meet at this convention tonight."

Bris

"The Covenant"; a ritual circumcision ceremony observed on a boy's eighth day of life.

"At a *bris*, even I get squeamish when the *mohel* picks up the instruments."

Bupkes

Nothing, or an insultingly disproportionate remuneration compared to expectations and/or efforts (said with scorn, sarcasm, or indignation).

"Can you believe this Fortune 100 company wanted me to coach their executives for *bupkes?*"

Chutzpah

Classic usage: gall, brazenness, nerve.

"It takes a dose of *chutzpah* to initiate conversations." RoAne's usage: Courage, gutsiness.

"The crook embezzles from the company and then requests a farewell party! That's *chutzpah!*"

Dreck

Trash, junk, that of inferior quality; a vulgar term not to use around my mother—or yours.

"When the *Wall Street Journal* describes some of what is available in cyberspace as *cyberdreck*, it must really be awful!"

Fe! or **Feh!**

An exclamatory expression of disgust and distaste.

"They are serving pasta with scallops and kumquats? *Feh!*"

Glick Luck or fortune.

"You should have *glick* in life."
(zoulzein mit glick).

Kibbitz To joke, fool around; to socialize aimlessly.

"The group in the corner of the room were *kibbitzing* over coffee."

Klutz A clod; a graceless person.

"Run a marathon? I am such a *klutz*, I'm lucky if I can step off a curb without spraining my ankle."

Kosher Fit to eat, ritually clean, trustworthy, proper, ethical.

"Using e-mail to fire a person is not *kosher.*" (Neither is bacon, shrimp, or lobster.)

Kvell To beam with immense pride and pleasure.

"The happy parents were *kvelling* at their son's bar mitzvah."

Kvetch To fuss, gripe, complain. Or, as a noun, the person who does that.

"Brenda is constantly *kvetching* about everything."

Maven An expert; knowledgeable person.

"With the explosive use of cell phones, the manners *mavens* have their work cut out for them."

Mazel
Luck.

"This book could be called *Make Your Own Mazel.*"

Mazel tov!
Good luck, congratulations.

"I am so pleased that you were promoted. *Mazel tov!*"

Megillah
Anything long, complicated, boring. The Purim story of Queen Esther.

"Tell me the results of the negotiations. I don't want to hear the whole *megillah.*"

Mensch
An honorable person of integrity; someone of noble character with a sense of sweetness as well as what is right and responsible. To call someone a *mensch* reflects deep respect.

"Mark Chimsky, my dear friend and advisor, is a real *mensch!*"

Nosh
To eat between meals. A snack, a small portion, a nibble.

"When someone prefers to *nosh,* it is known as 'grazing' in some quarters."

Nudge
To pester, nag; to give a surreptitious reminder of a job to be done.

As a noun, the person who is a nag (Pronounced *noodge*.).

"He kept *nudging* her to stop smoking."

Oy vey!   A lament, a protest, or a cry of delight; expresses anguish, joy, pain, revulsion, regret, relief.

"*Oy vey!* It is such a tragedy to lose a home in a fire. Thank heaven the family is safe."

Schlep   To drag, pull, or lag behind. Someone who looks bedraggled.

"Don't *schlep* all those packages; you'll hurt your back."

Schmooze   Friendly, prolonged conversation; act of chatting *with* someone.

"Ira and Michael *schmoozed* for an hour at the party." *Incorrect:* "Ira *schmoozed* Michael at the party."

Schnorrer   A cheapskate, a chiseler.

"That *schnorrer* orders a $100 bottle of wine and always manages to be in the bathroom when the check arrives.

Shtick   A studied, contrived piece of "business" employed by an actor (or salesperson); a trick; a devious trick.

"Watch him use the same *shtick* on this new client."

Shvitz

To sweat. As a noun, a steambath, where one goes to sweat (off a few pounds).

> When describing a very humid, summer day in New York that made her sweat, Katie Couric said it was her favorite word to say (rather than do).

Schmaltzy

Corny, mawkish, hackneyed emotionalism.

> "His *schmaltzy* comments about how wonderful the company has been to him made even the boss uncomfortable."

Tchotchke

A toy, a trinket, a knickknack.

> "I refuse to buy my clients *tchotchkes* with my logo plastered on them."

Tush

Derriere.

> "One cannot work a room on one's *tush*."

Yenta

Classic definition: A gossipy woman who does not keep a secret. It may also refer to a man who does the same.

Newer usage: Since *Fiddler on the Roof,* a matchmaker.

> "I do expect that in the next production of *Fiddler,* Yenta will sing 'Networker, Networker . . . make me a match.'"

Notes

CHAPTER ONE

1. Adair Lara, *San Francisco Chronicle*, p. D1.
2. Edna Gunderson, *USA Today*, April 7, 2003.

CHAPTER THREE

1. David Kirkpatrick, *Fortune*, Oct 13, 2003.
2. Vannessa Hua, *San Francisco Chronicle*, June 27, 2003.
3. *Psychology Today*, November/December 2003.
4. *Psychology Today*, March/April 2002, p. 74.

CHAPTER FOUR

1. *Marin Independent Journal*, November 29, 2003.

CHAPTER FIVE

1. AAA of Northern California, *Via* magazine, p. 25.
2. *San Francisco Chronicle*, October 10, 2003, p. E13.
3. Beth Ashley, *Marin Independent Journal*, August 29, 2001.

CHAPTER SIX

1. Sam Whiting, *San Francisco Chronicle Magazine*, August 10, 2003, p. 4.

CHAPTER SEVEN

1. Chip Johnson, *San Francisco Chronicle*, November 17, 2003.

CHAPTER EIGHT

1. David Perlman, *San Francisco Chronicle*, October 10, 2003.
2. Daniel Rosenberg, *Wall Street Journal*, October 3, 2003, p. A12.
3. CNETNews.com, September 27, 2003, online.
4. Cecilia Rasmussen, *Los Angeles Times*, September 21, 2003, p. B4.
5. *USA Today*, September 15, 2003.

CHAPTER NINE

1. Pete Barlas, *Investors Business Daily*, May 15, 2003.

RESOURCES

Barabasi, Albert-Laszlo. *Linked: The New Science of Networks.* Boston: Perseus, 2003.

Bronson, Po. *What Should I Do with My Life?* New York: Random House, 2002.

Butler, Pamela E. *Talking to Yourself.* San Francisco: Harper, 1981.

RoAne, Susan. *How to Work a Room.* New York: Harper Resource, 1988, 2000.

Wiseman, Richard. *The Luck Factor: Changing Your Luck, Changing Your Life.* New York: Miramax, 2003.

INDEX

For Those Desperately Seeking Susan

A speech is within your reach! To book best-selling author and in-demand **keynote speaker** Susan RoAne for your meeting, retreat, or convention,

Call:	415-239-2224
E-mail:	Susan@SusanRoAne.com
Mail:	The RoAne Group
	320 Via Casitas, Suite 310
	Greenbrae, CA 94904
Fax:	415-461-6172
Visit:	**www.susanroane.com**

To purchase Susan's print books or audio books, visit your local bookstore, online bookstore, or www .800CEOREAD. Or call 1-800-CEO-READ.

- *How to Work a Room®*
- *The Secrets of Savvy Networking*
- *What Do I Say Next?*
- *RoAne's Rules: How to Make the RIGHT Impression* (CD or audio only)

Additional speech topics include:

- How to Create Your Own Luck: Turning Serendipity to Success
- Super-NATURAL Selling
- Connect! The Personal Touch in a Digital World: How to Reclaim It

Do you have your own great You Never Know! story? Please email to: youneverknowbook@susanroane .com or send to The RoAne Group.